Preface

Research for Cultural Sensitivity Constructs and framework is multidimensional. It's a young discipline. The book focuses on recommendations for two areas that will help improving the education statistics overall.

1. Focus on early childhood schooling. Increasing access to early childhood education is another way countries can help prepare students for academic progress later on. For example, OECD research finds that in most countries, 15-year-olds who have attended pre-primary education tend to perform better on the OECD's PISA assessment than those who have not, even after accounting for students' socio-economic backgrounds.

2. Teachers' Instructional Practices, Participation in Professional Development, and Career Satisfaction.

The purpose of the Organon is to develop the skills and abilities required to be culturally competent. The outcomes of the program will allow participants to apply specific methods and strategies related to cultural competency within the context of their work either as:
1) a community member working with law enforcement and other organizations with authority
or,
2) an educator serving students in diverse communities with the perspective of protecting and advocating for students of color.

Additionally, providing a statistical system for findings and suggestions based on the prevailing issues faced and ways to improve the primary motive, i.e. public safety and rights of all along with the mentioned areas.

The book therefore tries to include what every educator and legislator needs to know. I would very much enjoy hearing what works and what doesn't.

Finally, this book is dedicated to my son Nieem Greenaway. I am deeply grateful for being your dad.

—Shuayb Greenaway
director@jegnaga.org
www.jegnaga.org
Philadelphia, PA
January 31, 2021

Chapter 1
Decoding The Cultural Logic of Education Manual

Learn to keep the door shut, keep out of your mind and out of your world every element that seeks admittance with no definite helpful end in view.
-George Mathew Adams

Jegna Global Alliance
director@jegnaga.org

Abstract

The long-lasting positive value of a high-quality early childhood education (ECE) is not in doubt among early childhood education practitioners, and researchers in the field. However, there is no standard definition of what a high-quality ECE is, what elements comprise it, or how to deliver such an education.

This manual fills that gap for all practitioners of ECE, both novice and experienced, as well as parents and other child caretakers who are interested in giving their children the best possible start in life. Starting from exploring the (usually unfunded) place of ECE in the United States' Public School System, the manual progresses to discuss the basis of high-quality early years education by presenting four foundational principles - the uniqueness of each child; the need for strong relationships; creating environments that enable; and development and learning. An additional principle that underlines the other four - cultural competency - is presented in some detail and flows through the entire manual.

Alongside the theoretical discussions, the manual presents many practical activities and exercises for putting these principles into practice. As superior ECE is highly individualized to each child, four key issues are brought into focus the children's diverse needs; partnerships that create value; flexibility needed to meet these needs; and aspects of play.

Another essential part of high-quality ECE is that of continuous improvement of every aspect of the process. This manual contains a detailed discussion of both the theory and the practice of accomplishing this.

The final part of the manual considers essential and integral requirements for the children's safety and welfare in an ECE environment. The manual gives practical suggestions as to the contents of a custom safety and welfare policy, and an overview of all the elements, including selecting suitable personnel that make up a safe and secure ECE environment.

Keywords: high-quality early childhood education, manual for ECE, how to deliver early childhood education, individual child education, superior early years education manual, manual children's education, cultural competence in education

Contents

1. INTRODUCTION

Research studies have shown that one or more years of high-quality early childhood education have a significant and lasting positive effect on a child's life - educational, social, and psychological - even up until the age of 15 years. However, not many researchers or ECE practitioners have addressed what the components of a high-quality early years education are or how to deliver such an education.

This manual describes what high-quality ECE would look like and presents practical actions that Early Childhood Education (ECE) providers can take to deliver individualized, high-quality education to the children in their care. It is intended for both novice and experienced ECE providers as well as parents and other caretakers of children who are interested in giving their children the best possible start in life.

The first part of this manual sets the scene by exploring where early childhood education fits into the public school system in the United States, as well as its importance. Four principles of high-quality ECE are discussed the uniqueness of each child; strong relationships; environments that enable; development and learning - along with the fifth principle of cultural competency that we present as the foundational principle to all forms of education and that can be introduced at this early stage. The first part of the manual continues with detailed advice on how to put these principles into practice by focusing on four key issues - children's diverse needs; partnerships; flexibility; and play. The section concludes by rounding out the elements of a high-quality early childhood education program with a discussion of quality improvement obtained through a continuously improving environment.

The activities and experiences in a high-quality ECE that support the children's development and learning growth are the focus of the second section of this manual. Four topics that facilitate planning, execution, and assessment are covered: early learning goals; observation; supportive practice; and plans and resources.

The third part of the manual concerns the requirements for the children's safety and welfare that should be met by the early childhood education providers. Developing a custom safety and welfare policy is the central focus here, with suggestions as to the kinds of events and circumstances that the policy document should contain. In addition, this section contains a review of what to look for in, and how to assess, suitable people to work with the children.

Throughout this manual, the skill

of cultural competency is an integral part of the philosophy, activities, and assessment of the early childhood education view that we present.

2. EARLY CHILDHOOD EDUCATION (ECE)

2.1. Public school

In the United States, there is no federal mandate for operating and maintaining public schools; each state has the responsibility for education within its boundaries, as detailed in its state constitution. This responsibility extends to setting and regulating the curricula, the teaching methods, and the teaching materials in the schools. This results in each state potentially having different policies, standards, quality, and content of the education available there [1, 2].

The state may delegate some of its authority to local school districts. In this case, the local education authorities work from a base curriculum framework provided by the state to develop their own curricula. The result of this may be diverse education opportunities available within one state. Many local school districts offer courses and activities beyond those mandated at the state level.

Kindergarten or Grade 1 is the first grade in which children enroll (between the ages of 5 and 8) in the mandatory public school system. Each state has different regulations for this.

2.2. Early childhood education options

Prior to this, the children may have experienced one of several optional early childhood education settings. These choices range from being cared for in the home through part-time attendance at a day care in which the focus may be solely socializing to the formal classroom-based learning environment of pre-Kindergarten classes. Many options offer some mix of academic, social, emotional, and physical learning and development activities; others, such as Montessori schools, order formal, structured early childhood programs.

While there is usually some state legislation concerning the licensing and implementation of some standards for some of these early childhood education settings, there is no regulation over the subjects and activities taught in them.

However, early childhood education providers can find guidance if they consider some principles for the delivery of development and learning education to the children in their care.

2.3. The importance of early childhood education

The value of early childhood education at a national level has been identified by The Organization for Economic Co-operation and Development (OECD). Although their list of reasons explains why countries should invest significantly in early childhood education for their youngest people, these reasons apply equally to the investment by a state in ECE or even by parents to pay for their child to attend a private early childhood education institution if public ECE schooling is not available to them [3].

Significant social and economic payoff Generates social and economic benefits now and in the future, for the individual, and for society.

More return for the investment

Children learn more and faster in the early years than in later school years.

Lasting impact

Positive effect of one or more years of quality pre-schooling still seen at age 15 years.

Multi-factored achievement

Despite socio-economic level and mother's education as factors, years at pre-school are as influential on children's academic achievement as years at elementary school.

Disadvantaged children benefit most

Disadvantaged children can catch up intellectually and socially with their more advantaged peers.

Societal benefits

Children who receive quality ECE are generally healthier and more risk-averse, leading to lower healthcare costs.

2.4. High-quality ECE

High-quality early childhood education is necessary to realize all the benefits of education for children in the early year's stage. There is no standard widely accepted definition of this or list of what elements go to make up a high-quality ECE program. Quality is often measured by looking at how the children in the program are progressing towards their intellectual, physical, social, and emotional goals. However, it is left to the ECE provider to determine which goals and criteria to put into the assessment.

Research shows that one or more years of high-quality early childhood education has a positive effect through-out the child's educational life. However, those who attended low-quality ECE programs were no different in what they achieved in school from the children who did not attend any form of ECE program [3, 4].

2.5. Four principles

The recognition of these four principles enables early childhood education providers to successfully support the development, learning, and welfare of young children in their early years [5].

2.5.1. Uniqueness

From birth, each child can be a competent learner who can demonstrate resilience, confidence, self-assurance, and capability.

2.5.2. Strong relationships

A secure and loving relationship with parents or an-other key person in each child's life encourages them to become independent and strong.

2.5.3. Environments that enable

The environments surrounding each child can actively be created to support and enable their development and learning.

2.5.4. Development and learning

All areas within each child's development and learning are interconnected and are equally important. Early childhood education providers should realize that each child develops and learns at different rates and in different ways.

We argue that behind these four principles is a fifth, that of cultural responsiveness, as demonstrated through cultural competence.

2.6. Cultural competence

Schools increasingly reflect the many cultural, ethnic, and racial groups in the US. Everyone needs to learn to successfully live within this cultural diversity. Be-ginning in the early year's stage, early childhood education programs can begin to teach children the skills of cultural competency so that they grow up being able to establish successful intercultural relationships and communication.

Cultural competence consists of four inter-related elements [6]:

2.6.1. Awareness

An examination of individual and other people's values, beliefs, and attitudes with respect to their own and others' cultures. Often these beliefs and attitudes hide stereotypes and prejudices that might be deep-seated and even unconscious.

2.6.2. Attitude

The more strongly held these differing beliefs and opinions, the more emotionally people respond to view-points from different cultural groups. Valuing the difference in cultures is an important part of moving towards cultural understanding.

2.6.3. Knowledge

By acquiring knowledge of different cultures, people are able to avoid "doing the wrong thing" in cross-cultural interactions. Building strong relationships involves understanding people and their lives, and knowing about even part of their culture helps to forge cross-cultural bonds.

2.6.4. Skills

Understanding your own cultural biases, valuing cultural diversity, and knowing about other cultural groups go a long way to cultural competency. But you still need skills with which to manage all of this. Knowing how to put the awareness, attitude, and knowledge into practice, and doing so, will enable you to manage cross-cultural difference.

2.7. Putting the principles into practice

The four principles can be effectively put into practice by focusing on four key issues: children's diverse needs; partnerships, flexibility; and play [5]. This focus gives early childhood education providers a solid foundation to meet the development and learning needs of the children in their care.

2.7.1. Children's diverse needs

Recognizing that each child is different, the provider should plan for the child's individual needs and deliver personalized learning and care. The primary goal is to give each child the best possible start in life.

Providers should be aware of obstacles or barriers to a child's learning - whether leading to the underachievement of some children or to hindering gifted children - and counter or possibly remove these. Identifying needs that might lead to learning difficulties is another responsibility that providers have.

Cultural diversity means that each child has their own values, attitudes, and beliefs, whatever culture they are from. If the ECE environment has an implicit policy of respecting each child and adult as a valued person, then valuing cultural differences should come quite naturally. Identifying the European-American students as a cultural group, along with any other cultures represented in the class, will emphasize that everyone belongs to a cultural group with its own values, beliefs, and traditions.

While each child has their own individual needs, some groups may have particular and specific needs. For example, children from ethnic minority groups, including those who have to learn English as another language, have their own culture and language needs. Children who have learning disabilities or difficulties have additional obstacles to deal with.

Teaching children to have positive attitudes to difference and diversity, especially with their classmates, is an important part of meeting diverse needs.

Making sure that each child values the different aspects of their own lives and of those of other children's lives is a start to their appreciation of the similarities and differences. Providers should challenge any discrimination or stereotyping they see or hear from a child or from an adult.

Showing respect for all children and adults, treating everyone as a valued individual, and making everyone feel included and safe are some ways to demonstrate, by example, positive attitudes and non-discrimination.

2.7.2. Partnerships

Partnerships between providers and other professionals, such as health and social workers, as well as with the child's parents or caretakers are key to responding quickly and effectively to any difficulties and concerns. This is important for all children, but notably for those with learning difficulties or other obstacles to deal with.

Even when there are no difficulties to address, providers should provide ongoing information to parents in various ways, such as by discussion, showing examples of the child's work, or through photographs.

2.7.3. Flexibility

Some children may not attend school consistently within regular school hours. Part-time attendance in one or more schools or time spent in before- and after-school clubs affects the planning and the resources needed to cover these varied schedules. In addition, one child may not be able to concentrate for long periods while another may become tired in the middle of the afternoon. Being aware of each child's schedule and their attention cycle allows providers to plan the day to deliver the most effective learning experience.

2.7.4. Play

Play is the vehicle for all development and learning for younger children. Children develop creatively, intellectually, socially, emotionally, and physically through play. Children play spontaneously and behave in various ways during play. For example, they may be boisterous and physical in running and jumping; they may describe and discuss what they are playing by telling a story, and they may be quiet as they play alone. All ways are valid and valuable play.

Two forms of child's play area of note: child-initiated and adult-led. In both forms of play, it is important to include both indoor and outdoor play activities. Different games and activities are possible outside and serve to keep the child interested as well as to ensure some physical exercise in the child's day.

Child-initiated. Play activities chosen by the child and carried out by them are called child-initiated. These activities often reflect the child's current interests. Playing with a truck on the floor and creating a route for it through the furniture is one example; telling a story about the dog they saw eating ice cream on the street is another. Child-initiated play may include imagination or using a toy or an object in a new way, such as using a watering can give the cat a drink. The early childhood education provider should show interest in child-initiated play activities and support them, perhaps by providing related resources.

Adult-led. For successful learning, child-initiated play activities should be balanced by adult-initiated ones, and it is up to the provider to decide the suitable balance of these for each child. Adult-initiated activities should be well planned and based on the child's spontaneous play and current interests. These activities can introduce a new skill or idea to the child. For young children, play may be watching a demonstration of a skill, perhaps putting toys away, the first few times and then they can take over the activity as they learn. Adult-led small group activities offer children the opportunity to interact by playing together in a supervised way.

Culturally inclusive play. Inclusion in any form is essential to a child-centered ECE program. Cultural inclusion is an important aspect of a culturally responsive curriculum and can be incorporated in many ways. All children should be included in all aspects of school life. Teaching children about cultural awareness can include activities that reveal both cultural similarities and cultural differences within the classroom group as well as in the outside world. Observing cultural holidays and traditions is a fun way to bring in aspects of culture from the home; comparing how birthdays are celebrated can help the children start to value the cultural differences.

Play should include culturally diverse practices [7]. Introducing the children to games and methods of play from different cultures widens their toolbox of play techniques and also gives them different opportunities to design games for themselves. Making a game of teaching the children to correctly pronounce each other's names highlights that they are all valued as individuals and as group members.

Providers and play. For both kinds of play, the provider should provide a challenging environment to enable the child to learn something new or to build on something they already know. Developing a child's language ability is a key element of play and the child should be encouraged to communicate about the play activities. The provider also has a role in the child's spontaneous play, in that, by observing and reflecting on what the child is doing and is interested in, they can create more fun and valuable play sessions.

Play benefits. By playing in a protected and challenging environment, with adult support where needed, children can:

feel safe to take risks and make mistakes as well as to explore

learn and make sense of the world through building up ideas, concept, and skills, and practicing them

use their imaginations and think

creatively learn problem-solving skills

communicate with others.

2.8. Quality improvement

The value of high-quality educational experiences in a child's early years should not be underestimated. The successful learning experiences a child has, at school, at home, and elsewhere, have a significant positive impact on their social, emotional, and cognitive development. This aids their progress through school and in their adult life.

A high-quality learning experience is one that provides learning and development support specifically designed for each child. Having high expectations and effective practices improve the outcomes for every child and provide a base for future success. The parents' or other caretakers' involvement is an important contribution to the continued quality of the experiences.

2.8.1. Characteristics of a continuously improving setting

The most important element of high-quality provision of early years care is the quality of the stakes. As always, providers should value each child as a unique individual, respect diversity, and offer individualized, personal learning.

The lead early childhood education provider and the sta should possess specific qualities and understanding.

The lead provider should:

support continuous improvement by example, showing enthusiasm and energy for the process

employ a holistic approach, looking at the whole setting

support collaboration in the working environment, the learning culture, and the group expression of the shared pedagogical objectives

recognize the importance of

and encourage continuous improvement, by consulting with local authorities, experts (consultants, teachers, etc.) on the subject

commit to quality practice by using (or creating) the quality improvement tools available, (such as self-evaluation forms and various rating scales)

work with the sta to generate a culture of reflective practice and self-evaluation through informed discussions to identify the strengths and priorities for continuing to improve the quality of care provision

work with the sta to identify their own continuous professional development needs.

The sta should:

have appropriate and up-to-date training and qualifications, and a willingness for self-development in their profession.

work collaboratively in the learning setting to share knowledge and test new ideas, take part in scheduled cycles of review and planning and share best practices

work collaboratively beyond their work setting through local, regional, and even national networking and attendance at conferences

support the continuous quality improvement process by recognizing its value to the children's continued development

engage in self-reflection practice and critique both their own performance and the development and learning processes themselves

balance adult-led and child-led activities to develop sustained shared thinking that will extend each child's thinking and enable them to make connections in learning.

work in partnerships with parents and other stakes, involving them as appropriate in the child's continuous learning. This is especially important in periods of transition between settings or from one setting to elementary school.

2.9. Secure environment

In a process of continuous quality improvement, the environment should be secure and stimulating. Elements to create such an environment include

a space that promotes physical, emotional, and mental health and well-being enough space, preferably outdoors, for the children to explore and in which to be physically active

flexible and changeable physical organization spaces within the larger space to accommodate personalized learning for all children, including those with special educational needs

an environment that has a continuity of care that enables children to develop substantial relationships with key workers.

2.10. Transitions

The continuity of care within a process of continuous quality improvement should extend to transitions between different settings.

Transitions are a process, not an event, and should be planned for and discussed with the children and their parents or caretakers. Meeting the children's social, emotional, and educational needs at these times is essential for the continued establishment of a firm foundation for their future success.

The personnel in the receiving setting (perhaps kindergarten or Grade 1 in elementary school) should use the child's summative assessment from their previous setting to plan for their first year. Once again, partnerships between providers, parents, and any other key people are important for a successful transition.

3. DEVELOPMENT AND LEARNING

The development and learning requirements of the early childhood period cover activities and experiences that support the children's growth in their development and learning in the years before they attend elementary school. The requirements include the goals - educational, social-emotional, and interpersonal - that the children should reach by the end of the period so that they are ready for kindergarten or Grade 1.

An important element of development and learning is a continuous assessment carried out by the early childhood education provider to measure each child's progress against their individual goals and to plan for future growth. As always, an environment of care and feeling valued is key to providing optimal development and learning opportunities.

Development and learning can be split into four topics to facilitate planning, execution, and assessment: early learning goals; observations; supportive practice; and plans and resources.

3.1. Early learning goals

Achievement of the early years learning goals of each child depends, in large part, on the developing knowledge, attitudes, understanding, and skills that they learn.

The early childhood education provider should set out what these necessary achievements are.

The children's goals should not be age-related, as different children progress at different rates through the stages in different ways. Movement from one stage to the next involves building on and expanding the achievements of each child and what they continue to practice and refine.

In the US, there are no social learning goals for children in the early childhood period to meet before they enter kindergarten or Grade 1. Neither the federal nor the state governments are involved in curriculum setting for early childhood education.

However, there is plenty of information available to assist early childhood learning providers in setting both goals and programs for the children in their care. Many organizations and individuals - school textbooks publishers, education providers, parents, Departments of Education in other countries (Canada and UK, for example), and so on - have published, on the Internet, advice, and lists of skills and knowledge,

they consider suitable and useful for children at the end of the early year's development and learning period. In researching this, providers can develop both qualitative and quantitative goals for the children.

The learning and development goals set at the end of the early years learning period may include specific educational subjects as well as social-emotional competencies and interpersonal relationships.

Here is one example from the UK Government [5]. This model breaks the learning goals for the end of the early childhood period into sections:

Communication and language

Listening and attention
Understanding
Speaking

Physical development

Moving and handling themselves
Health and self-care regarding physical exercise and nutrition; also basic hygiene

Personal, social, and emotional development

Self-confidence and self-awareness
Managing feelings and behavior
Making relationships

Literacy and Mathematics

Reading

Writing

Numbers

Shape, space, and measures

Understanding the World

People and communities the world

Technology

Expressive arts and design

Exploring and using media and materials being imaginative.

3.2. Observations

Ongoing regular and frequent (daily or weekly) observation of each child, noted and recorded in a standard format, is necessary to assess the progress the child is making. Knowing what the child is easily learning along with where they are struggling allows the early childhood education provider to adjust the individualized learning plan for that child.

Early identification of any learning or development concerns enables the provider, parents, and anyone else involved in the education process to create and put into practice a revised plan to quickly begin to address those concerns.

Closely observing the child enables the provider to understand the child well and to develop a positive relationship with them, as well as with the parents or care-takers. Identifying a child's changing or emerging interests allows the provider to continually develop relevant play and learning activities in the child's learning plan.

At the end of the early childhood period, some children will have reached their goals while others will still be working toward theirs.

3.3. Supportive practice

Supportive and effective practice in children's early year's development and learning is a combination of everything discussed so far along with the four principles discussed earlier. Daily observational assessment, properly recorded, will form a view of where the child is currently in their learning, where they need to go, and how to get them there. For the learning practice to be effective, it should be constant and consistent, and the providers should be supportive of all aspects of the process.

3.4. Plans and resources

Producing an individualized plan for every child and amending that plan based on the child's changing interests, progress in development, and the available re-sources requires careful planning and an ability to respond to changes in circumstances. Learning plans should also be flexible enough to accommodate the spontaneous interest of a child in an unexpected event, such as a rainbow after a storm or the first frost of fall.

For a child's learning to be successful, exciting, and varied, providers in a team can draw from each other's knowledge and experiences when developing the plans for the children in their care and in creating a successful learning environment. Providers working alone and not in a setting with other caregivers should be especially attentive to networking opportunities for feedback and information sharing.

3.5. Assessment

To support high-quality development and learning, providers should work to continually improve their processes for delivering education. Assessments, to know the current level of quality, are a crucial part of a continuously improving ECE setting.

Continuous improvement, planning, and informed decision-making require effective and regular assessment of each child's progress in their development and learning. Assessment for learning is a regular assessment activity that uses a standardized form and a standard scale to assess each child similarly.

Assessments should also be performed for the environment; the program; the processes; and the sta. Given the importance of a culturally responsive learn-in curriculum, a cultural assessment, or audit, is a way to assess the cultural competencies of the learning environment through its sta and programs.

3.5.1. Cultural audit

An ECE organization can have cultural competence; this is the sum of the cultural competencies as seen in its sta, its programs, and the results as shown in the children's learning within a culturally responsive curriculum. Conducting the first cultural audit gives a base-line view of where the ECE organization is, and subsequent audits give time-stamp snapshots of any improvements made to the level of cultural competency. The cultural audit identifies the difficulties and opportunities that have arisen in managing cultural diversity. Continuous improvement is obtained through evaluating the audit and addressing the gaps found in the cultural awareness, attitude, knowledge, and skills.

3.5.2. Children's assessment

Assessing each child's progress towards their development and learning goals provides key information for continuous improvement, informed decision-making, and planning.

Two types of children's assessment should be an integral part of a successful learning environment.

Formative assessment. The formative assessment guides everyday planning. In this assessment, the early childhood education provider regularly observes the child (daily, weekly) understand the child's level of achievement and their learning styles and interests. The provider uses observations, videos, photographs, things the children have made, and also includes information from parents and other caregivers. In short, anything from the everyday environment of the children.

Summative assessment. This is a summary of the child's activities and progress towards their learning goals over a long period. The provider writes the summative assessment by summarizing the formative assessments for the child. The summative assessment may contain all relevant records, discussions with parents and other caretakers, and input from any other adult who can make a useful contribution. The child's progress against the learning goals should be discussed.

Summative assessments are usually passed on to the next phase of the child's learning journey, perhaps elementary school. Such a summary gives the elementary school teacher an idea of who the child is and their current abilities, as well as assists in the elementary class planning.

As early childhood education is usually optional (except for kindergarten in some states), it does not fall under the realm of either federal or state governments. Therefore, standardized assessment forms are not common.

However, a quick search on Google brings up a selection of websites (and Pinterest boards) that contain suitable pre-school assessment forms (both formative and summative) from teachers, parents, education providers, and others that could be useful to providers in developing a custom assessment form.

Cultural considerations. The children's assessment form should reflect the ECE's philosophy of valuing cultural diversity. The assessment criteria, especially for the formative assessment, should take into account culturally specific behaviors and communication styles for all the children in the ECE program.

4. CHILDREN'S SAFETY AND WELFARE REQUIREMENTS

The children's welfare should be of prime concern to providers. The welfare and safeguarding requirements cover how providers must keep children safe and promote their welfare.

Every child deserves to be healthy, secure, and safe, and children learn best when they are in such an environment. This welcoming and stimulating environment also enables the child's individual needs to be met and lets children create positive relationships with the adults who care for them.

To ensure the children's welfare, early childhood education providers should safeguard the children; ensure that adults who have contact with the children are suit-able; promote good health; manage behavior; and keep complete records, policies, and procedures.

4.1. Children's welfare policy

The legal requirements of safeguarding a child's welfare when they are being cared for are set by each state. The requirements vary from state to state but mostly cover such matters as sta; environment; physical space; organization; equipment; and documentation and reporting.

While early childhood education providers should be knowledgeable about all the legal requirements for their state, they should also create and write their own policy document that explains how they safeguard and promote the welfare of the children in their care.

The custom Children's Safety and Welfare policy document should include, but need not be limited to, the following sections:

4.1.1. Personnel

The roles and responsibilities of the individual providers and of the managers.

The name of the person who has the lead responsibility for safeguarding the children; this provider might have responsibility for liaising with local government departments and agencies.

The key person assigned to each child; this provider is responsible for ensuring the child receives individualized care.

4.1.2. Concerns about a child

The training that is available to recognize signs of abuse or neglect in a child and how to raise a concern about such a child.

What to do when a concern about a child's safety or welfare is raised; how this will be recorded.

How to refer these concerns to the appropriate local government department (children's services; social services; the police, etc.).

4.1.3. Allegations against sta

The procedure to follow if an allegation is made about a volunteer or a sta member.

4.1.4. Information sharing

How to inform parents of the content of this policy manual before they place their child.

When and how to inform parents about any concerns for their child and about any actions taken.

How confidentiality is managed.

4.1.5. Sta training

How the sta's knowledge of child safeguarding measures will be kept up to date.

4.2. People involved

4.2.1. Key person

Each child in the child care setting must be assigned a key person. The primary responsibility of the key person is to ensure that each child's care is individualized to their particular needs. In addition, the key person helps the child settle into the setting, offers a continued and secure relationship with the child, and builds a relationship with the parents or caretakers.

4.2.2. Suitable people

Providers must have effective systems in place to ensure that the people who encounter the children are suitable to fulfill the requirements of their role. The high quality of the children's daily experience in a caregiving situation depends on all the sta having the appropriate qualifications, skills, knowledge, and training, as well as a full understanding of their roles and responsibilities.

Childcare workers must meet education and training requirements, which vary by state and sometimes by local region. However, here are some key issues to be aware of:

License. Most, but not all, early childhood care providers need to have a license from their state or local government [8]. Some child care providers who may be exempt from the licensing requirements include relatives of the child they care for, those caring for a small number of children, and those who provide care for only a few hours a day.

Licensing, however, is not a guarantee of quality; it just sets minimum standards and monitors programs to ensure that providers comply with them. Child care licensing regulations are different from state to state and may cover some or all of the following topics, and more:

the child-sta ratio and the maximum number of children in a group

the safety of the physical location, such as cleanliness, emergency exits, and any potential dangers to the children

procedures to be put in place to stop the spread of disease, including those surrounding diapering, handwashing, and immunizations the nutrition of the food served to the children, including information about allergies and a limit on the number of sugary snacks training and other requirements for the sta working at the child care program.

The National Database of Child Care Licensing Regulations [9] has contact information and a link to state websites for the state licensing department. In addition, many states keep a record of child care licensing inspections in the records on their website.

Background checks. The early year's child care provider is responsible for the safety and well-being of the children in their care. To this end, the lead provider must make sure that all adults (sta and some volunteers) who have access to the children have had a comprehensive background check. The provider will examine each background check to ensure that the adult does not have a recorded history of violence or child abuse [8].

The people who should provide background checks include teachers; caregivers; bus drivers; janitors; kitchen sta and administrative employees. Volunteers who have unsupervised access to the children also need to provide background checks.

Cultural competence. The first step towards assessing the cultural competence of the people who work with the children is to ask the sta to assess their own cultural biases, stereotypes, and prejudices. This is often a di - cult and disturbing task, especially when performed for their own culture as well as for other cultures. However, understanding personal cultural biases, even if they cannot let them go, is a step towards understanding their influence on cross-cultural communication and interactions.

Training and education. The training and education - including health and safety training - of the child education providers should be appropriate for the setting and for the ages of the children. The following topics are useful skills and areas of knowledge for providers to have:

Children's first aid and CPR

child development, physical activity, and nutrition

prevention and recognition of child neglect and abuse

prevention and control of infectious diseases (including immunizations)

use and dispensing of medication

food allergies; prevention of emergencies

emergency preparedness and responses for disasters, natural and otherwise hazardous materials -handling, disposal and storage

safety on the premises - indoor and outdoor transporting children safely.

Providers should also be able to meet the health and safety requirements (including in emergencies) of children with special needs. ECE providers may also need additional training in specialist areas to obtain these skills and knowledge.

4.3. Quality of care

While being licensed does not guarantee the quality of a caregiving establishment, some states offers a quality rating and improvement system (QRIS) for child care programs [10]. Participation in QRIS, if available, may be optional or mandatory. Early childhood programs that do participate earn higher ratings as they meet more quality standards. The QRIS rating is one way of accessing the quality of early years learning pro-vided. The National Association for the Education of Young Children offers accreditation for early childhood programs if they meet the 10 program standards set out by them [11, 12].

4.4. Premises

The safety, security, and suitability of the premises, including all outdoor spaces, must be continuously maintained. Spaces, equipment, toys, and furniture must be appropriate and safe for the ages of the children. All the space and equipment must be kept clean and up to any standards identified in the appropriate state's health and safety legislation.

Procedures for emergency evacuation should be in place and well documented. Appropriate fire detection equipment should be in good working order, as should fire extinguishers and other control equipment. Fire exits should be clearly marked and fire doors should be kept clear and be easily opened. Everyone should know where the muster point is.

References

1. Findlaw. (2019) The roles of the federal and state governments in education. Retrieved from https://education.findlaw. com/curriculum-standards-school-funding/the-roles-of-federal-and-state-governments-in-education. html
2. Corsi-Bunker, A. Guide to the education system in the United States. Retrieved from https://isss. umn.edu/ publications/education/
3. OECD. Investing in high-quality early childhood education and care (ECEC). Retrieved from https://www.oecd.org/ education/ school/48980282.pdf
4. Vandell, D.L. (2010) Do effects of early child care extend to age 15 years? Results from the NICHD

study of early child care and youth development. Journal of Child Development. 81 (3).

5. Vaughn, B. (2007). What is cultural competence and how is it measured? San Francisco: DTUI Publications Division. Retrieved from https://diversityofficermagazine.com/cultural-competence/what-is-cultural-competence-how-is-it-measured-2/

6. Lynch, M. (2014). 6 ways teachers can foster cultural awareness in the classroom. Retrieved from https://blogs.edweek.org/edweek/education_futures/2014/11/6_ways_teachers_can_foster_cultural_awareness_in_the_classroom.html

7. GOV.UK (2014). Early year's foundation stage pro-File: exemplification materials. Retrieved from https://www.gov.uk/government/publications/eyfs-profile-exemplication-materials

8. Childcare.gov. Childcare licensing and regulations. Retrieved from https://www.childcare.gov/consumer-education/child-care-licensing-and-regulations

9. National Center on Early Childhood Quality Assurance. National database of child care licensing regulations. Retrieved from https://childcareta.acf.hhs.gov/licensing

10. National Center on Early Childhood Quality Assurance. About QRIS. Retrieved from https://qrisguide.acf.hhs.gov/about-qris

11. National Association for the Education of Young Children. NAEYC Early learning program accreditation standards and assessment items. Washington, DC: NAEYC. Retrieved from https://www.naeyc.org/sites/default/files/ globally-shared/downloads/PDFs/accreditation/early-learning/standards_and_assessment_web_0. pdf

12. National Association for the Education of Young Children. The 10 NAEYC program standards. Retrieved from https://www.naeyc.org/our-work/families/ 10-naeyc-program-standards

Chapter 2
Decoding The Cultural Logic of Education

Know or listen to those who know.
-Baltasar Gracian

Jegna Global Alliance
director@jegnaga.org

Abstract

Quality early childhood education (ECE) delivers a solid foundation on which a child's intellectual, psychological, emotional, and physical development can build.

Measuring the quality of early childhood education can be as straightforward as regularly assessing a child's developmental and learning progress towards their individual goals. However, determining the elements within ECE that contribute to a high-quality education program for children in their early years is not as easy.

One way of ensuring ECE is of the required quality is to develop early childhood education programs based on four principles: uniqueness of each child; strong relationships; enabling environments; and ongoing development and learning.

The authors argue that another essential principle to high-quality early childhood education is cultural responsiveness. This principle underlies the other four principles throughout ECE. A high-quality ECE program will develop the skill of cultural competence in both the ECE providers and in the children, through creating a culturally inclusive curriculum. Cultural competence starts with cultural awareness to recognize and accept cultural diversity and then teaches how to value the cultural differences. The competence part comes in with the teaching of skills with which to manage these cultural differences to build successful intercultural communication and relationships.

This paper explains what ECE is, describes the five principles, and details how they can be effectively put into practice in three key areas to provide high-quality ECE: development and learning practices; assessment; and children's safety and welfare.

Keywords: early childhood education, cultural competence, high-quality ECE, culturally responsive early childhood development, cultural diversity in ECE

5. Early childhood education

5.1. Public education

In the United States, public education is operated, regulated, and maintained by the individual states. The primary role of the federal government is to establish policy for and administer federal assistance to education and to collect data about US schools. Each state's constitution details how its responsibility to education is to be carried out: designing and regulating curricula; deciding what teaching methods and teaching materials are to be used; the accreditations the teachers require, and so on. The state may delegate some of this authority and responsibility to local school districts that then build on a base curriculum framework to develop their own teaching plans. This decentralization of responsibility for education results in different states, and even schools, districts within a state, having different education policies, quality, standards, and content of education [1, 2].

Kindergarten or Grade 1 of elementary school (depending on the state regulations) is the first mandatory grade that children attend within the public school system. This occurs between 5 and 8 years of age.

5.2. Early childhood education (ECE)

5.2.1. Early childhood education settings

Prior to entering the mandatory public school system at the elementary level, children may have optionally experienced one of several early childhood education (ECE) settings. The most common definition of the early years period is between birth and 5 or years old when children start public school; however, the United Nations Educational, Scientific and Cultural Organization (UNESCO) extends this definition to 8 years old, which is usually when children are in Grade 3 [3].

Options available for early childhood education cover a continuum from children being cared for at home through daycare to pre-school to pre-schools with for-mal, specialized programs such as Montessori. Attendance can be part-time or full-time, one or more days a week, and from birth onwards in the case of home care and daycare. The activities and learning experiences within these settings may be solely focused on socializing or may include some measure of academic learning along with social-emotional and physical development activities.

A useful explanation of early childhood education, as opposed to daycare, is that early childhood education uses experiences and activities to positively effect developmental change in children in the early year's stage.

The learning goals of early childhood education are to create hands-on and active learning experiences in a positive pre-school environment to provide a social, academic, and social-emotional foundation for young children in their lifelong learning.

This is accomplished through planning education programs that develop and nurture the physical, psychological, and social well-being of the children and their families.

As early childhood education is not mandatory, it is not the responsibility of either the local school authorities or the state. However, some states do provide free pre-school education. Otherwise, the parents or caretakers of the children pay for the cost of attendance at such institutions. There is commonly some state legislation concerning the licensing and implementation of some standards for some of these early childhood education settings, there is no regulation over the subjects and activities taught in them.

5.2.2. The importance of early childhood education

The early childhood years are increasingly recognized as the first stage in a child's lifelong learning journey. Creating a solid developmental foundation at this time creates a base for educational, social, and family policy agendas [4]. How, when, and to whom ECE is available reflects the nation's or state's cultural and social beliefs about young children, the roles of families, and the commitment to investing public money in sup-porting education from an early age.

The Organization for Economic Co-operation and Development (OECD) provides a list of reasons why countries should invest in early childhood education for their youngest citizens [5]. These reasons, however, apply equally to the investment by a state in early education or even by parents to pay for their child to attend a private early childhood education institution if public ECE schooling is not available to them.

Significant social and economic payoff

In business terms, the early childhood education costs today will generate benefits in the future, both economic and social, for the individual and for society as a whole. The individual child will benefit from strong social-emotional skills throughout their life and in adulthood from a higher income due to their education as they develop an early solid foundation that carries them

28

through all their educational levels. Society will benefit from an increased tax base and more informed citizenship.

More return for the investment

Before the age of three, a child's brain is in its most sensitive stage of development. Language and number ability, social skills with peers, and emotional control all peak before or during a child's third year. Children learn more and faster at this early childhood stage than in later life. Investing in early childhood education through pre-school programs generates a higher return on investment (ROI, in business terms) than the same investment spent on later schooling.

Lasting impact

The educational impact of early childhood education shows up clearly by the age of 15-years. OECD's Programme for International Student Assessment examined students who were 15 years old and found that those who had attended one year or more of pre-school scored higher in reading, by 30 points or more, than those who did not.

Multi-factored achievement

Many factors affect child dev-elopment and learning, not least of which is the child's home environment. Also in the mix are socio-economic factors (including family income) and the mother's level of education. But putting these aside, a study in the UK found that, at age 11, children's educational achievement was as influenced by their few years at pre-school as it was by their many more years at elementary school.

Disadvantaged children benefit most

Disadvantaged children have the greatest chance to develop their skills in early childhood education. These children are generally less developed, both academically and socially, when they start kindergarten or Grade 1 directly. They have more opportunity to catch up when enrolled in ECE. This narrows the achievement gaps and places them on a more equal footing with their more advantaged peers.

Societal benefits

Studies have shown that children who receive early childhood education are generally healthier and have a reduced need to carry out risky behavior. They also engage more in social interactions, including at the community level. These advantages translate on a societal level to lower health costs and more socially engaged citizens.

5.2.3. Not just any ECE

In much of the advice, research, and reports published about early childhood education, high-quality early childhood education is assumed, either explicitly or implicitly. Not run-of-the-mill development and learning, but high-quality programs. The next section address what such a program looks like.

5.2.4. High-quality ECE

Asking what high-quality early childhood education generates a variety of answers. There is no standard or widely accepted definition or list of quality elements. Furthermore, any definition would have to be content- and culturally specific and be open enough to change over time.

UNICEF provides a general definition of how to measure quality in ECE [6]:

"Fundamentally, quality in pre-primary education is measured by how well the learning environment supports children in gaining the knowledge and skills that will enable them to develop intellectually, physically, socially, and emotionally."

Children's developmental outcomes are often the criteria by which quality is measured. However, there is still the question of which outcomes to use in the assessment. Educational organizations sometimes give a a suggested list of goals that children should reach before they finish their early childhood education [7].

Unicef also points out that quality ECE is the sum of many interlinked components, including teachers, communities, families, quality assurance, resources and planning, and an inclusive child-centered curriculum. All of these components need to be present and of sufficient quality to contribute to a high-quality program.

Along with child development results, other elements of a high-quality ECE could include the child-sta ratio; sta qualifications; material resources; process quality including sta-child interactions; and so on [8].

5.2.5. The importance of high-quality ECE

Research shows the positive effects of high-quality early childhood education. A study by the US National Institute for Child Care monitored children in several states and found that, at the age of 15, those who had received high-quality early childhood education had the most positive educational achievements [9]. A similar study in the UK found that the quality of pre-school education still exerted a positive influence on literacy and math even after the children had been in elementary school for five years [5].

However, the children who had been to ECE settings of low quality were no different in their educational achievements from those who had not attended any form of pre-school.

In summary, ECE providers and researchers seem to agree that a high-quality early childhood education is important in giving children the best start in their educational, social, psychological, and physical lives. However, it is still unclear what a high-quality ECE program should look like.

The rest of this report offers some suggestions of what a high-quality early childhood education program should contain and some ideas of how to deliver that level of quality.

6. How to deliver high-quality ECE

Early childhood education providers agree that high-quality ECE can be recognized by the development and learning progress of the children in the educational setting. However, how to deliver education that facilitates the necessary attainments is where the challenge lies.

Research studies suggest that high-quality ECE encompasses four principles: uniqueness, strong relation-ships, environments that enable, and development and learning. Building an educational program based on these principles provides a solid foundation to delivering high-quality ECE.

The rest of this report looks at three key areas of such an educational program – development and learning (how to deliver the program); assessment (know where you are and where you need to progress); and child welfare and safety (keeping them safe, secure and health) – and discusses how to achieve high-quality education in each area.

But first, we start by arguing that an integral, necessary, and key component of a high-quality early childhood education program is cultural competence. Cultural competence (also known as cultural sensitivity) should be built into all elements of an ECE program from the beginning, from sta self-reflection to curriculum development to the children's activities to the criteria used to assess the program and processes.

6.1. Cultural competence

Cultural competence is an essential skill for early childhood education providers to possess and to teach to the children in their care. Schools increasingly reflect the many cultural, ethnic, and racial groups in the US. Everyone needs to learn to successfully live within this cultural diversity and, beginning in early childhood, pre-schools can play a significant role in teaching this.

With different backgrounds - languages; values; beliefs; rituals; celebrations; and so on - it can be di cult for people to understand and to communicate with each other. This can lead to misunderstandings and a lack of trust or, alternatively, can lead to valuable learning experiences and shared knowledge of different cultures appreciated and valued by everyone.

6.1.1. Awareness, valuing, and competence

Cultural awareness is the first step to cultural competence. This is an awareness that different cultures have similarities and differences. Valuing this cultural diversity is an attitude that leads to understanding that the different elements found in each culture can provide value to the group as a whole, and are in themselves valuable.

Both cultural awareness and valuing cultural diversity generate knowledge about different cultures, of both the similarities and differences. But neither offer advice on how to deal with the cultural differences [10]. Cultural competence builds on both of these to provide skills to manage the cultural differences and to facilitate effective cross-cultural interactions.

6.1.2. Four elements of cultural competence

Cultural competence has four inter-related elements [10]:

Awareness recognizes diversity-related beliefs and values, especially, perhaps unconscious, deep-down prejudices and stereotypes. These can create barriers for teaching as well as for learning and development.

Attitude relates to how strongly people hold these differing opinions and beliefs. The more strongly held they are, the more emotionally people react to and even dismiss culturally different viewpoints. Valuing cultural diversity comes in here.

Knowledge about different cultures provides points of connection in cross-cultural interactions. For example, knowing the communication style of someone from a different culture allows a person to not feel threatened at a more aggressive form of talking than found in their own culture.

Skills are necessary to manage cultural difference. They bridge the gap between knowing about the cultural differences and being able to build successful intercultural relationships.

6.2. Four principles of high-quality ECE

High-quality early childhood education is identified with four principles. Basing the ECE on these principles allows providers to support, in the early years, the successful development and learning of children.

Uniqueness recognizes that all children from birth can be competent learners, with confidence, resilience, self-assurance, and capabilities.

Strong and secure relationships with parents or alternative key people in children's lives encourage the children's independence and self-confidence.

Environments that enable and support children's development and learning can be actively created and maintained.

Development and learning is an ongoing process in which all the areas are interconnected and of equal importance. Each child learns and develops in different ways and at a different rate to their peers.

All four of these principles work together to provide the necessary foundation to develop a high-quality early childhood education program in three key areas.

6.3. Development and learning practices

Development and learning practices provide many opportunities to put the four principles into practice in facilitating high-quality early childhood education.

Within development and learning, the four principles can be effectively put into practice by focusing on four key issues: children's diverse needs; partnerships, flexibility; and play. This focus gives early childhood education providers a solid foundation to meet the development and learning needs of the children in their care.

6.3.1. Children's diverse needs

Each child is different and providing child-centered education requires the provider to plan for each child's individual needs. Delivering personalized learning and care contributes greatly to ECE's primary goal of giving each child the best possible start in life.

To create the individualized programs, providers need to be aware of any obstacles or barriers to the child's learning and to remove or nullify them. Such barriers may be leading to underachievement by some children or beholding gifted children back.

Whatever culture they are from, the children have their own values, beliefs, and attitudes. They may also have different communication styles. Teaching cultural awareness to children starts their cultural competence program. If the early childhood education setting has an implicit policy of respecting and valuing each person, then valuing these cultural differences should fall naturally into everyday life. When identifying the different cultural groups the children belong to, identifying the European-American students as such a group, with its own values, traditions, and beliefs, will reinforce that it is another cultural group like the others.

Even while each child has their own unique needs, some groups may have particular and specific needs. For example, children from ethnic minority groups will have their own cultural needs, including the need to learn English as another language. In addition, children who have learning disabilities or difficulties have additional obstacles to deal with. All of these diverse needs should be taken into account when planning the development and learning activities and goals.

Another important part of meeting children's diverse needs is to teach them to have positive attitudes to difference and diversity, especially with their classmates and sta members. Starting with an awareness of cultural differences and similarities (these are just as important) between their own life and the lives of their classmates, children can learn to appreciate and value each person and to learn about all the varied lives going on around them. Equally important is that providers should set an example of non-discrimination by challenging any dis-crimination or stereotyping they hear or see from a child or from an adult.

Demonstrating respect for everyone (children and adults alike), treating everyone as a valued individual, and making everyone feel safe and included are some ways to show positive attitudes and non-discrimination by example.

6.3.2. Partnerships

Partnerships are the key to responding quickly and effectively to any difficulties and concerns. Partnerships can be between ECE providers and other professionals, including health and social workers, as well as with the child's parents. Forging such strong relationships is in the interests of all the children, but especially so for those with learning different or other obstacles to deal with.

Even when everything is going well, the ECE provider's relationship with the child's parents or care-takers should be maintained. Providers should regularly give the parents or caretakers updates about their child in various forms – discussions, samples of the child's work, photographs of the child doing an activity, and so on.

6.3.3. Flexibility

It is important, and di cult, to manage early child-hood education settings when some children, or their parents or caretakers, do not have regular schedules. But the flexibility to provide non-standard hours of education is an important element to providing high-quality ECE.

Some irregular schedules may be: not attending school every day regularly; part-time attendance in one or more schools; early start or late pick-up needed. Scheduling issues may arise within a day: one child may be able to concentrate for only short periods or another may become sleepy in the middle of the afternoon. All of this requires flexibility in scheduling activities and events, even to an individual level; and this requires juggling resources and materials.

Being aware of each child's schedule and their attention cycle allows providers to plan the day to deliver the most effective learning experience.

6.3.4. Play

Successful development and learning in the early childhood years depends greatly on the play. By playing, children develop their creative, social, emotional, and intellectual skills as well as develop physically. Playing spontaneously allows children to behave in many different ways. For example in running and climbing, they are boisterous and physical; in describing what they are doing they use their story-telling and descriptive abilities; and by playing alone, they may prefer to be quiet. All of these ways are valuable and valid expressions of play.

Two forms of play are important in high-quality early childhood education: child-initiated play and adult-led play [7]. In both of these, however, providers should encourage and provide opportunities for both indoor and outdoor activities. Outdoor play is especially important in allowing for physical play and activities.

Child-initiated. Child-initiated play occurs when the child chooses and leads the play activity. These activities are useful for providers and others to observe as they often reflect the child's current interests. Examples of child-initiated activities include the child playing with a truck on the floor and finding a route for it through the obstacles of the furniture and the family dog; listening to the child excitedly tell a story about how they saw a cat chase a squirrel up a tree is another child-led activity. The child giving the cat a drink by using the flower watering can is a child-led activity that uses the child's imagination as well as finds a new use for an everyday object. Supporting child-led play, perhaps by providing additional resources, is one way to encourage such creativity.

Adult-initiated. Child-initiated play should be balanced by adult-initiated play for optimum development and learning results. The ECE provider should decide for each child what the best balance of the two methods is. Observing children's spontaneous play allows the provider to tailor the planned adult-led play to each child's interests. The ECE provider can introduce a new skill or idea through play, or build on existing skills and knowledge. First demonstrating the new skill several times allows the child to learn at their own pace before they attempt the activity on their own. Adult-led small groups provide opportunities for children to play together in a supervised and directed way.

Culturally inclusive play. Inclusion is an important aspect of cultural competence and the curriculum can be culturally inclusive in many ways. When developing the ECE curriculum, all children should be included in all aspects of the school life. Cultural awareness activities acknowledge and teach about cultural differences and similarities, within the classroom group and out in the world. Special activities and events, especially observed holidays and birthdays, encourage the children to incorporate their non-school life into the curriculum; this provides numerous opportunities to discuss cultural differences and similarities found in the home and else-where. All of this cultural awareness and cultural valuing activities should allow for different communication styles, even making that the subject of investigation or discussion.

The activities and experiences of early childhood education, especially play, should include culturally di-verse practices [11]. For example, culturally responsive practices can build play activities to acknowledge and celebrate different languages and communication styles. This is an effective way to be sensitive to children who are learning English as another language. Introducing the children to culturally specific methods and preferences of play not only widens their toolbox of play techniques but also gives them more opportunities to express themselves in play. Ensuring that all the children can correctly pronounce each other's names shows that they are all valued members of the group.

Providers and play. For both child-and adult-initiated play, the early childhood education provider should provide a challenging yet secure environment. The children should feel safe to take the risks to learn something new or to build on something they already know. Developing a child's language ability is important in play and encouraging the children to communicate to each other and to the provider about their play activities strengthens this skill. Even when the children are involved in the child-initiated play, the ECE provider should be there to oversee and supervise; they also observe and reflect on what the children are doing, in order to incorporate these insights into the adult-initiated play sessions.

Play benefits. The benefits of children playing in a challenging yet protected environment, with adult support where needed, are numerous. They include creating a feeling of safety for the children for exploring and for taking risks and making mistakes; learning and making sense of the world by building up and practicing ideas, concepts and skills; playing imaginatively and creatively; learning problem-solving skills; and communicating freely with others.

6.4. Assessment

Continuous improvement is the hallmark of a high-quality early childhood education environment. To continually and consistently deliver high-quality early childhood education, providers should work to constantly improve their education delivery processes. The elements of a continually improving setting include collaboration in and beyond the learning environment; a culture of self-evaluation and reflective practice; partnerships with a parent, caretakers, and sta; and using quality improvement tools such as standard ratings and forms for assessment.

Assessment is a key component of continuous improvement. This includes an assessment of the environment; the program; the processes, the sta, and the children. With cultural responsiveness a key element to high-quality early childhood education, a cultural audit is also needed.

6.4.1. Cultural audit

Assessing the cultural competence of the early childhood education environment is a major element of continuous improvement. A cultural audit of the early year's education environment provides a baseline view of the cultural competencies within the education processes and of the sta themselves. Regularly conducting the audit gives a time-based snapshot of how these competencies are changing over time, due to improvement e orts.

The overall level of cultural competence reflects the level of knowledge, behavior, and attitudes related to skills used in managing cultural diversity. The cultural assessment identifies the opportunities and difficulties that have arisen or may arise in the future, due to cultural differences. Building a culturally competent organization requires evaluating the cultural audit and addressing the gaps and difficulties found in the cultural awareness, attitude, knowledge, and skills.

Children's assessment

Effective and regular assessment of each child's progress in their development and learning provides key information for continuous improvement, informed decision-making, and planning. Such assessment for learning should become a regular activity; using a standardized form, standard criteria, and a uniform scale ensures that each child is assessed similarly.

Two types of assessment should be an integral part of a successful learning environment:

Formative assessment. Formative assessment guides everyday resource planning and scheduling. In formative assessment, the ECE provider regularly observes the child (daily, weekly) and notes the child's achievements, and their learning styles and interests. Observations, videos, photographs, things the child has made, and discussions with parents and other caretakers provide this information. In short, the provider can draw on anything from the everyday life of the child in conducting the assessment.

Summative assessment. The provider writes the summative assessment at the end of a time to summarize the child's progress and achievements in respect to their individual learning goals. The summative assessment is basically a summary of the formative assessments.

It may contain all relevant records, discussions with the parents and any other caretakers, and information from any other adult who has something constructive to add.

The provider usually passes on the summative assessment to the next educational institution the child is to attend, usually kindergarten or Grade 1 in elementary school. Such a summary provides the new teacher or ECE provider with an idea of who the child is, their current abilities and interests, and assists them in class planning.

Standardizing the assessment. As early childhood education is usually optional (except for kindergarten in some states), it does not fall under the realm of either federal or state governments. Therefore, standardized assessment forms are not common.

But searching Google [try "Pre-school assessment form"] reveals a selection of websites (and Pinterest boards) that contain pre-school assessment forms (both formative and summative) from teachers and other education providers as well as from parents. These forms could be useful to providers in developing their own custom assessment forms.

Cultural considerations. Culturally specific behaviors and attitudes should be an explicit consideration when developing the assessment protocols for assessment forms, especially for formative assessment. Taking into account the different behaviors, values, and beliefs found in a culturally diverse early childhood education class when creating the measurement criteria ensures that the assessment is not measured solely against the behavior expected in US culture. This is another way to show by example that cultural differences are truly valued.

6.5. Children's safety and welfare

Of prime concern to early childhood education providers is the welfare of the children. Welfare and safeguarding requirements, some put in place by state legislation, cover how to keep the children safe and promote their welfare.

Every child deserves to be healthy, safe, and secure; children learn best when they are in an environment that promotes this. A welcoming and stimulating environment also enables each child's individual needs to be met and encourages children to create positive and strong relationships with the adults who care for them.

Ensuring the children's welfare involves establishing a policy that details how to safeguard the children. This includes checking that adults (sta and volunteers) who encounter the children are suitable. The children's good health should be promoted by managing their diet when they are in the ECE setting and by managing their behavior there as well. In addition, keeping complete records, policies and procedures ensures that any information needed about welfare and safety is always available.

Children's welfare policy

Legal regulations. Each state sets its own legal requirements for safeguarding a child's welfare when they are being cared for. The requirements vary from state to state but have elements in common including sta; the environment; the physical space; the organization; equipment; and documentation and reporting.

Early childhood education providers need to know about all the legal child welfare and safeguarding requirements for their state. However, they should also create and write their own policy document that explains how they promote the welfare of the children in their ECE establishment.

Custom policy document. When developing a custom policy document for the welfare and safeguarding of children, the ECE provider could consider including the following sections (and any others they deem necessary):

Personnel

The roles and responsibilities of the individual providers and managers.

The name of the person with lead responsibility for safeguarding the children; this provider might have responsibility for liaising with local government departments and agencies.

The names of the key person assigned to each child; this provider is responsible for ensuring the child receives individualized care.

Concerns about a child

The training that is recommended or available to recognize signs of neglect or abuse in a child; how and with whom to raise a concern about such a child.

What to do when you are concerned about a child's welfare or safety is raised; how to record this.

How and who to refer these concerns to (the appropriate local government department -children's services; social services; the police, etc.).

Allegations against adults

The procedures to follow if an allegation is made about a volunteer or a sta member.

Information sharing

How to inform parents of the content of the policy manual before they place their child.

How and when to let parents know about any concerns for their child and about any actions taken.

How the sta manages confidentiality. Sta training

How the sta will keep their knowledge of child welfare and safeguarding measures up to date.

6.5.1. People involved

Key person. Each child in the early childhood education setting must have a key person assigned to them. The primary responsibility of the key person is to ensure that each child's development and learning is individualized to meet their particular needs. In addition, the key person helps the child settle into the environment, builds a continued and secure relationship with the child, and develops a relationship with the parents.

Suitable people. ECE providers must have an effective system to ensure that the only people who meet the children are suitable to fulfill the requirements of their role. The high quality of the children's daily experiences in a caregiving situation depends on all the sta having the appropriate qualifications, skills, knowledge, and training. Childcare workers must meet education and training requirements, which vary by state and sometimes by local region. In addition, sta need a full understanding of their roles and responsibilities.

6.5.2. Elements of suitability

In assessing the suitability of the early childhood education setting and sta, here are some key elements to ask questions about and to look out for.

License. In all states, most, but not all, early childhood care providers must receive a license from their state or local government to operate. Child care providers who may be exempt from the licensing requirements include relatives of the child they care for, those caring for a limited number of children, and those who provide daycare for only a few hours a day [12].

Licensing, however, is not a guarantee of quality; it just sets the minimum standards and then monitors pro-grams to ensure that providers comply with them. Child care licensing regulations differ from state to state and may cover numbers such as the child-sta ratio and the maximum number of children in a class. Safety elements are usually covered such as the cleanliness of the premises, available emergency exits, and any potential dangers to the children. Health procedures could insist on specific needs surrounding diapering, handwashing, and imm-unizations. Health might also involve requirements for the nutritional com-ponents of any food served to the children and a limit to the number of sugary snacks. This component could also contain details of any information to be provided about allergies and what is to be done in the case of an allergy attack. A major component of the licensing requirements might be the training, experience, and other requirements for the sta working at the childhood education center.

The National Database of Child Care Licensing Regulations keeps contact information and has links to the state licensing department for each state. In addition, many states keep a record of child care licensing inspections in the records on their website [13].

Background checks. The ECE provider has responsibility for the safety and well-being of the children in their care. One aspect of this is that the lead provider must ensure that all the adults (sta and some volunteers) who have contact with the children have had a complete background check. The provider examines each background check to make sure that the adult does not have a recorded history of violence or child abuse [12].

The people for whom background checks are necessary include teachers; caregivers; bus drivers; janitors; kit-chen sta and administrative employees. Volunteers who have uns-upervised time with the children also must provide background checks.

Cultural competence. Suitable people to work with the children should possess a degree of cultural competence. The first step towards assessing this is for the early childhood education providers to address their own, often unconscious, cultural stereotypes, biases, and prejudices – not only for other cultures but also in their view of their own culture. It can be di cult to face personal ethnocentric beliefs and then to let them go or, at least, to be aware of them. Deep self-reflection may re-veal thoughts to not be proud of. However, understand-ing personal biases is a start to identifying how they may affect cross-cultural relationships with the children, their parents or caretakers, sta members, and with volunteers.

Training and education. All ECE providers should have received the training and education – including health and safety training appropriate for the setting and for the ages of the children. The following topics are useful skills and areas of knowledge for providers to have:

First aid and medical - children's first aid and CPR; dispensing medication; food allergies

Child development – development and learning; social-emotional; physical

Health - infectious diseases prevention and control (including immunizations); nutrition; food allergies

Safety - on the premises, indoor and outdoor; hazardous materials, handling, disposal, and storage; transporting children safely

Child welfare - prevention and recognition of child neglect and abuse

Emergency preparedness - responses for disasters, natural and otherwise.

ECE providers should also have the training and knowledge to meet the health and safety requirements of children with special needs, including in emergencies. Providers may need to attend specialist training to obtain these skills and knowledge.

6.5.3. Quality of care

The possession of a license by an early childhood education establishment does not necessarily guarantee the high quality of the education provided. However, some states offer a quality rating and improvement system (QRIS) for child care and early childhood education programs [14]. An ECE provider's participation in QRIS, if available, may be optional or mandatory in some states. Early childhood programs that do participate gain higher ratings because they meet more quality standards. The QRIS rating is one way of accessing the quality of early years learning provided.

The National Association for the Education of Young Children also offers an accreditation for early childhood programs if they meet the 10 program standards set out by them [15, 16].

6.5.4. Premises

Early childhood education providers have the responsibility to maintain the safety and security, and the suit-ability, of the premises. All indoor and outdoor spaces must be regularly maintained. Providers should ensure that spaces, furniture, equipment, and toys must be appropriate and safe for the ages of the children cared for. All the space and equipment must be kept clean and up to the standards, if any, identified in the appropriate state's health and safety legislation.

A major safety issue is the evacuation of the children in an emergency and procedures for this should be in place and well documented. For example, fire is always a major hazard. Fire extinguishers and other appropriate fire detection equipment should be in good working order. Clearly marked fire exits should be visible and fire doors should be kept clear and be easily opened. Every-one should know where the muster point is. Evacuation drills are highly recommended.

7. Moving forward

In the US and throughout the world, workplaces, schools, and communities increasingly consist of varied cultural, racial, and ethnic groups. This cultural diversity can broaden an individual's outlook, inspire creativity and drive innovation. People in diverse groups and teams collectively have a wider range of knowledge, values, and attitudes that can contribute to a common goal.

Attaining cultural competence, in which people learn to manage cultural diversity and build successful intercultural relationships and com-munications, can start at an early age. Providers of early childhood education should create a culturally inclusive environment, develop a culturally responsive curriculum, and ensure cultural representation in the activities and learning experiences for the early years children. Not only will early childhood education provide a solid foundation for a child's socio-emotional, physical and intellectual developmental and learning, but it will also prepare them to become successful global citizens and value the differences

43

and similarities in the diverse cultures that they will encounter throughout their lives.

References

1. Findlaw. (2019) The roles of the federal and state governments in education. Retrieved from https:// education.findlaw. com/curriculum-standards-school-funding/the-roles-of-federal-and-state-governments-in-education. htm

2. Corsi-Bunker, A. Guide to the education system in the United States. Retrieved from https:// isss.umn.edu/ publications/ USEducation/

3. UNESCO. (2019). Early childhood care and education. Retrieved from https://en.unesco.org/themes/ early-childhood-care-and-education

4. OECD. (2001). Starting strong: Early childhood education and care. Retrieved from https:// www.oecd.org/newsroom/ earlychildhoodeducationandcare. html

5. OECD. Investing in high-quality early childhood education and care (ECEC). Retrieved from https://www.oecd.org/ education/ school/48980282.pdf

6. United Nations Children's Fund. (2019) A world ready to learn: Prioritizing quality early childhood education. New York: UNICEF. Retrieved from https://www.unicef. org/ reports/a-world-ready-to-learn-2019

7. GOV.UK (2014). Early years foundation stage profile: exemplification materials. Retrieved from https://www.gov. uk/government/publications/ eyfs-profile-exemplication-materials

8. Allen, L., Weiss, R. A., Weiss, R. G. (2019). Transitions to school: What helps children succeed? Retrieved from https://www.apa. org/advocacy/education/ transition-to-school

9. Vandell, D.L. (2010) Do effect of early child care extend to age 15 years? Results from the NICHD study of early child care and youth development. Journal of Child Development. 81 (3).

10. Vaughn, B. (2007). What is cultural competence and how is it measured? San Francisco: DTUI Publications Division. Retrieved from https:// diversityofficermagazine. com/ cultural-competence/what-is-cultural-competence-how-is-it-measured-2/

11. Lynch, M. (2014). 6 ways teachers can foster cultural awareness in the classroom. Retrieved from https://blogs.edweek.org/edweek/ education_ futures/2014/11/6_ ways_teachers_can_foster_ cultural_awareness_in_the_ classroom.html

12. Childcare.gov. Childcarelicensingandregulations. Retrieved from https://www. childcare.gov/consumer-education/ child-care-licensing-and-regulations

13. National Center on Early Childhood Quality Assurance. National database of child care licensing regulations. Retrieved from https://childcareta.acf.hhs.gov/licensing

14. National Center on Early Childhood Quality Assurance. About QRIS. Retrieved from https://qrisguide.acf.hhs.gov/about-qris

15. National Association for the Education of Young Children. NAEYC Early learning program accreditation standards and assessment items. Washington, DC: NAEYC. Retrieved from https://www.naeyc.org/sites/default/files/ globally-shared/downloads/PDFs/accreditation/ early-learning/standards_and_assessment_web_0.pdf

16. National Association for the Education of Young Children. The 10 NAEYC program standards. Retrieved from https://www.naeyc.org/our-work/families/ 10-naeyc-program-standards

Chapter 3
Statistical and Analytical Report
on Cultural Sensitivity

Know or listen to those who know.
-Baltasar Gracian

Abstract

This research is conducted for a detailed recommendation report based on the areas of interest and priority of the organization as specified for setting up a statistical analysis system for the purpose of credentialing programs related to Cultural Sensitivity.

The areas of interest are prepared based on two credentialing programs: The Community Cultural Sensitivity Credential Program and the Instructor Cultural Sensitivity Credential Program.

The main motive of both the credentials are based on cultural sensitivity and competence which is basically a set of skills that enables people to learn about and understand people with a cultural background different from them. It deals with the behaviour and ways to effectively communicate with an individual with a different cultural orientation than us and make him/her feel accepted while doing so. This report compiles the findings and recommendations based on the areas of interest that are crucial for the maximum success of the credential program.

This report was commissioned by Jegna Global Alliance and they hold the intellectual property rights for it. Keywords: Culture, Diversity, Ethnicity, Cultural Sensitivity, Early Education

8. Introduction

8.1. Background:

8.1.1. Culture and Diversity:

Culture is a shared system of meanings, beliefs, values, and behaviors through which experience is interpreted and carried out. It largely affects how we view the world, family, relationships, and others.

Diversity is the mosaic of people who bring a variety of backgrounds, styles, perspectives, values, abilities, and beliefs as assets to the organizations and groups to which they belong. Dimensions of diversity can be age, ethnicity, language, sexuality, religion, race, gender, country of origin, etc.

8.1.2. Cultural Competence:

It is termed as an ability to interact effectively with people of cultural backgrounds. Developing cultural competence results in an ability to understand, communicate with, and effectively interact with people across cultures.

8.1.3. Cultural sensitivity in a professional environment:

Most businesses work with people from two or more different cultural backgrounds at the same time, it is important to pro-mote effective communication among employees and employers. Cultural diversity has its own limitations including both verbal and non-verbal methods of expressing things to one another in any social environment. Proper actions can make a lasting, positive impression and provide the recipient a feeling of Acceptance and ease.

8.2. Objectives:

The primary objectives of the cultural sensitivity credential program are to:

1. Make the participants be able to explain the difference between diversity, cultural awareness, and cultural competence.
2. Participants should be able to introspectively look at a situation, identify their position in the cultural awareness continuum and think of ways to progress to the next level.
3. Identify and discuss the cultural barriers from case studies and/or real-life situations.
4. To carry out item analysis and discriminant grouping

9. METHODOLOGY

9.1. Research Design

A part of the information for this report was sourced from publications by the US Government's public data at https://www.data.gov also proved valuable. This report is not a comprehensive review of the available literature but is an overview of the topic.

9.2. Tools used

The data from US Government public data records were analyzed and studied using the Python programming language along with Excel. Also, Data Ferrett provided by the US Central Bureau has been used.

9.3. Item Analysis:

Item statistics were used to assess the performance of individual test items on the assumption that the overall quality of a test derives from the quality of its items.

9.4. Mean and Standard Deviation

The mean is the "average" student response to an item. It is computed by adding up the number of points earned by all students on the item, and dividing that total by the number of students.

The standard deviation, or S.D., is a measure of the dispersion of student scores on that item. That is, it indicates how "spread out" the responses were. The item standard deviation is most meaningful when comparing items, which have more than one correct alternative and when scale scoring is used. For this reason, it is not typically used to evaluate classroom tests.

9.5. Item Difficulty

For items with one correct alternative worth a single point, the item difficulty is simply the percentage of students who answer an item correctly. In this case, it is also equal to the item mean. The item difficulty index ranges from 0 to 100; the higher the value, the easier the question. When an alternative is worth other than a single point, or when there is more than one correct alternative per question, the item difficulty is the average score on that item divided by the highest number of points for anyone alternative. Item difficulty is relevant for determining whether students have learned the concept being tested. It also plays an important role in the ability of an item to discriminate between students who know the tested material and those who do not. The item will have low discrimination if it is so di cult that almost everyone gets it wrong or guesses, or so easy that almost everyone gets it right.

To maximize item discrimination, desirable difficulty levels are slightly higher than midway between chance and perfect scores for the item. (The chance score for five-option questions, for example, is 20 because one-fifth of the students responding to the question could be expected to choose the correct option by guessing.) Ideal difficulty levels for multiple-choice items in terms of discrimination potential are:

Table 2.5. Ideal difficulty levels for Multiple-choice items

Question Format	Difficulty
Five response multiple choice	70
Four response multiple choice	74
Three response multiple choice	77
True or False	85

Item difficulty can be said as "easy" if the index is 85% or above; "moderate" if it is between 51 and 84%; and "hard" if it is 50% or below.

9.6. Item Discrimination

Item discrimination refers to the ability of an item to differentiate among students based on how well they know the material being tested. Various hand calculation procedures have traditionally been used to compare item responses to total test scores using high and low scoring groups of students. Computerized analyses provide a more accurate assessment of the discrimination power of items because they take into account responses of all students rather than just high and low scoring groups.

The item discrimination index provided is a Pear-son Product Moment correlation^ 2 between student responses to a particular item and total scores on all other items on the test.

This index is the equivalent of a point-biserial coefficient in this application. It provides an estimate of the degree to which an individual item is measuring the same thing as the rest of the items.

9.7. Alternate Weight

Multiple correct alternatives may be assigned a different weight.

9.8. Test Statistics

Two statistics are used to evaluate the performance of the test as a whole.

The reliability of a test refers to the extent to which the test is likely to produce consistent scores. The particular reliability coefficient computed reflects three characteristics of the test:

Interco relations among the items — the greater the relative number of positive relationships, and the stronger those relationships are, the greater the reliability. Item discrimination indices and the test's reliability coefficient are related in this regard.

Test length — a test with more items will have higher reliability, all other things being equal.

Test content — generally, the more diverse the subject matter tested and the testing techniques used, the lower the reliability.

Reliability coefficients theoretically

range in value from zero (no reliability) to 1.00 (perfect reliability). In practice, their approximate range is from .50 to .90 for about 95% of the cultural tests. High reliability means that the questions of a test tended to "pull together." Students who answered a given question correctly were more likely to answer other questions correctly. If a parallel test were developed by using similar items, the relative scores of students would show little change. Low reliability means that the questions tended to be unrelated to each other in terms of who answered them correctly. The resulting test scores reflect peculiarities of the items or the testing situation more than students' knowledge of the subject matter.

As with many statistics, it is dangerous to interpret the magnitude of a reliability coefficient out of context. High reliability should be demanded in the cultural certification since the test score is used to make major decisions. The measure of reliability used is Cronbach's Alpha. This is the general form of the more commonly reported KR-20 and can be applied to tests composed of items with different numbers of points given for different response alternatives. When coefficient alpha is applied to tests in which each item has only one correct answer and all correct answers are worth the same number of points, the resulting coefficient is identical to KR-20.

10. STATISTICAL ANALYSIS AND INTERPRETATIONS

Upon analysis of available data, the following statistics were found out for various cities of America:

10.1. Statistical findings of Baltimore City

Total Population: 602,495

10.5.2. Educational Attainment:

10.5.3. Educational Attainment by Race:

10.5.4. Language Spoken by proportion:

10.5.5. Employment Rate by Age:

10.5.6. Unemployment Rate by Age:

10.5.7. Employment Rate by Race:

10.5.8. Unemployment Rate by Race:

10.5.9. Poverty Rate by Race:

10.6. Statistical Crime reports

10.7. Access to Healthcare

Racial and Ethnic Minorities are less likely to have a regular doctor and health insurance. They are less likely to obtain preventive services, or diagnosis, treatment, and management of chronic conditions. Health insurance coverage is also an important determinant of access to health care. Higher proportions of minorities compared to Whites do not have a usual source of care and do not have health insurance (see Figures 3.7.A and 3.7.B).

11. FINDINGS

11.1. Stages of cultural sensitivity:

The first stage defines ethnocentrism as the attitude or point of view by which the world is analyzed according to the parameters of our own culture. It often involves the belief that one's own ethnic group is the most important, or that some or all aspects of our culture are superior to those of other cultures. The stages of ethnocentrism are:

Denial: recognizing cultural differences perceived by the naked eye (schedules, holidays, food, dress, etc.) but denying deeper intrinsic differences.

Defense: criticizing other cultures with negative or derogatory terms as a result of feeling threatened, which leads to negative stereotypes, prejudices, and discriminatory attitudes.

Minimization: thinking that values and behavior are universal principles and are equal to one's own.

The second stage is ethno relativism,

a learned skill, where a person consciously recognizes values and behaviors as a cultural matter rather than a universal one. The stages of ethno relativism are:

Acceptance: recognizing that cultural differences must be respected in order to improve interactions we may not agree with a specific cultural practice or difference but we respect a co-worker's values.

Adaptation: to be able to change a cultural outlook or behavior, which improves understanding and communication in different cultural contexts.

Integration: an e ort to integrate different cultural elements and feel comfortable with multi-cultural situations.

Only upon passing all these stages can an individual be claimed to have attained cultural competence. The concept of developing intercultural sensitivity reflects that our perception is flexible, and we all have the ability to reformulate our sensitivity according to new experiences.

11.2. Benefits:

11.2.1. Community Cultural Sensitivity Credential Program:

In a community, cultural sensitivity is needed for better communication and the development of interpersonal relationships. It is of prime importance

Baltimore Median Age

35	33.7	36.2
Total	Male	Female

Baltimore Sex Ratio

Female	328,419	52.99%
Male	291,377	47.01%

Race	Population
Black or African American	389,222
White	187,725
Asian	15,855
Two or More Races	14,387
Some Other Race	10,412
American Indian and Alaska Native	1,886
Native Hawaiian and Other Pacific Islander	309

Table 3.1.1. Population of people by race in Baltimore

as it is the platform where people need to interact with other individuals from different cultural backgrounds and make decision

The main aim of such programs are to make people aware of the different cultural backgrounds and also make the line of communication clear between people who lack a common cultural platform. These programs can help people to:

1. Learn about themselves: It can help people acknowledge their culture and viewpoints and hence helps them clear out their mind for the further process.

2. Overcome the cultural barriers: In any social meeting, there always exists some barriers such as preconceptions, stereotypes, and prejudices which hinder the flow between people.

3. Trust building: When the cultural understanding is present among the individuals, there is a formation of trust between both parties. And once

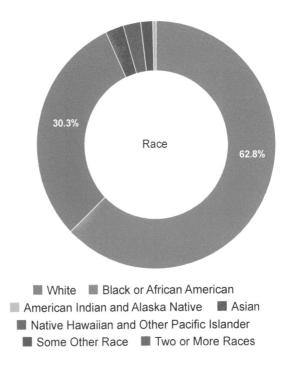

30.3%

Race

62.8%

■ White ■ Black or African American
■ American Indian and Alaska Native ■ Asian
■ Native Hawaiian and Other Pacific Islander
■ Some Other Race ■ Two or More Races

Figure 3.1.1. The proportion of people by race in Baltimore

the trust factor is created, all the altruistic tendencies seem to play a pivotal role.

4. Career development: It helps an individual enhance the skills as well as a knowledge base to a great extent. They become eligible as well as confident to take up different positions in companies across the globe.

5. Promotes confidence: When individuals and teams have an understanding of each other's culture, they get a self-confidence factor while dealing with each other.

11.2.2. Instructor Cultural Sensitivity Credential Program:

Culturally responsive teaching is an approach that empowers students intellectually, socially, emotionally, and politically by using cultural referents to impart knowledge, skills, and attitudes.

This program can help instructors and widely benefit the education system:

1. Acknowledge the legitimacy of the cultural heritages of different ethnic groups, both as legacies that affects students' dispositions, attitudes, and approaches to learning and as worthy content to be taught in the formal curriculum.

2. Use a wide variety of instructional strategies that are connected to different learning styles and are mostly organized around low-pressure, student-controlled learning groups that can assist in the development of academic language.

3. Instructors employ active learning methods and are designed to promote student engagement by requiring that students play an active role in crafting curriculum and developing learning activities.

4. A Culturally Responsive Curriculum is authentic, child-centered, and connected to the child's real life. It employs materials from the child's culture and history to illustrate principles and concepts.

5. Build bridges of meaningfulness between

Education Attained	Count	Percentage
High School Graduate	126,395	29.72%
Some College	82,107	19.31%
Bachelors Degree	67,779	15.94%
Graduate Degree	61,584	14.48%
9th to 12th Grade	46,577	10.95%
Less Than 9th Grade	20,732	4.88%
Associates Degree	20,061	4.72%

Table 3.1.2. Education attainment details for people in Baltimore

home and school experiences, between curriculum and social reality.

6. Incorporate multicultural information, resources, and materials in all subjects routinely taught in schools.

7. Students are allowed to control some portion of the lesson, providing instructors with insight into the ways that speech and negotiation are used in the home and community.

11.3. Challenges:

While dealing with a cultural sensitivity problem, there can be a lot of challenges such as:

1. Each culture has its own conventions for every action. People communicate with one another based on their culture that establishes correct tempo & tone of voice. For example, some cultures start discussions with specific detail; others with generalities.

2. Although all cultures value respect, they may communicate respect differently which can be misunderstood by a person of another culture. Trust, or lack of trust has an effect on intercultural communication. Commonly, the use of humor can be easily misinterpreted and can negatively affect communication (especially puns and sarcasm).

3. Different understandings of professional etiquette, i.e. a person's personal preference of way of eating food, eating habits, religious beliefs and norms of society might differ and conflict from others. In such cases, people should make an e ort to understand and accept the logic of other cultural frame-works and take it as a creative opportunity.

4. Professional communication can be misinterpreted or di cult to understand across languages and cultures.

12. CONCLUSIONS AND RECOMMENDATIONS

Taking into consideration the benefits and challenges in dealing with a culturally diverse environment, the key points to be considered are:

12.1. Language Barriers:

Most of the cities taken into consideration in the U.S. have a high proportion of English speaking population as compared to other ethnic groups. While communicating with each other, there is a high possibility of language becoming a major barrier.

Listening is one of the most important

aspects of effective communication. It involves not just understanding what the speaker is saying, but also understanding how the speaker feels about what they are saying.

Effective listening can make the speaker feel heard and understood as well as create an environment where everyone feels safe and avoid negative emotions.

12.2. Low literacy:

Low literacy widely affects access to health care. The 1992 National Adult Literacy Survey found that 40 to 44 million Americans do not have the necessary literacy skills for daily functioning. The elderly typically have lower levels of literacy, and have had less access to formal education than younger populations. Older patients with chronic diseases may need to make multiple and complex decisions about the management of their conditions. Racial and ethnic minorities are also more likely to have lower levels of literacy, often due to cultural and language barriers and differing educational opportunities. Low literacy may affect patients' ability to read and understand instructions on prescription or medicine bottles, health educational materials, and insurance forms, for example. Those with low literacy skills use more health services, and the resulting costs are estimated to be $ 32 to $ 58 billion — 3 to 6 percent — in additional health care expenditures.

12.3. Emotional awareness:

There is a large proportion of white race people in comparison to other races (Black, Hispanic, Asian, etc.) except for Detroit which has a high population of Black people. When the population comprises of a large

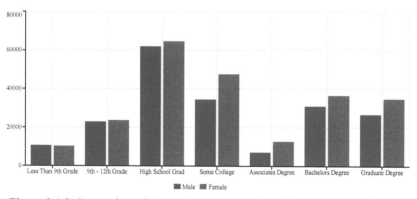

Figure 3.1.2. Proportion of education attainment level by gender in Baltimore

majority, it is important for every individual to acknowledge emotional awareness so as to not hurt anyone or get hurt by each other's actions/ behavior in a social scenario. Emotional awareness is the ability of an individual to manage their feelings appropriately.

Emotional awareness helps to understand and empathize with what is really troubling other people. It also helps in self-realization, including the cause of the trouble.

Stay motivated to understand and empathize with the person you're interacting with, even if you don't like their message.

Communicate clearly and effectively, even when delivering negative messages.

Build strong, trusting, and rewarding relationships, think creatively, solve problems, and resolve conflicts.

12.4. Conflict Resolution:

Stereotypes are one of the major causes of conflicts. Stereotypes are often pejorative (for example Italians al-ways run late), and can lead to distorted expectations about your counterpart's behavior as well as potentially costly misinterpretations.

A second common reason for cross-cultural conflicts is that people tend to interpret others' behaviors, values, and beliefs through the lens of our own culture. In order to overcome this tendency, it is important to make people aware of the other party's culture. It should include not only researching the customs and behaviors of different cultures but also, understanding why people follow these customs and exhibit these behaviors in the first place.

12.5. Adjusting to Differences:

Differences are common in any social environment and should not be considered as a barrier to cross-cultural communication at an organization or an institution.

The major points to be followed to incorporate difference cultures are:

Infusion of culture, language, and equity content in coursework so that each individual has knowledge about cultural differences.

Focusing on culturally responsive, equity-focused pedagogy

Preparation to teach English language learners

Name	Total	High School	Bachelors
Black	256,145	209,644	39,618
White	133,681	119,709	73,771
Hispanic	17,221	11,776	4,585
Asian	11,294	10,294	8,219
Multiple Races	6,858	6,234	2,904
Other Race	6,174	4,284	1,524
Native American	1,232	995	221
Islander	253	253	74

Table 3.1.3. The population of people and their educational
attainment by race in Baltimore

Developing cultural knowledge
and sensitivity

Learning advocacy beyond the
classroom

12.6. Guidance for State Leaders

1. Use information that is relevant
   and no older than 3 years
2. Cross-domain information
   modelling is important
   when working with cultural
   sensitivity.
3. Analysis of matters should be
   carried out keeping correlation
   of state airs in mind.
4. Minority groups should be
   encouraged to participate in

academic as well as extra-
curricular events.
5. A total population of the
   minority should be sampled
   carefully when carrying out
   state reforms. This includes
   minorities' poverty ratio,
   employment ratio, and
   education attainment ratio.

12.7. Eight Areas of Performance Assessment for Competency

12.7.1. Methodology

The goal of competency assessment
is to identify potential problems with
the certification program and to help
the state to start with a clear and clean
process. Observations followed by

documentation of remediation are critical components of the competency assessment process.

12.7.2. Application

The following application procedure ensures the correct assessment of competency.

12.7.3. Objective

The following procedure describes how to assess the competency.

12.7.4. Responsibilities

The Director is responsible for:

Ensuring the implementation and supervision of certification competency assessments;

Taking any required action as indicated by the assessment results.

The Quality Manager assigns appropriate sta as Competency Assessors.

The Competency Assessors are responsible for conducting the competency assessments and documenting the results.

An observer is advisable if there is sufficient sta.

12.7.5. Areas of performance assessment:

1. Political Understanding - Political Savviness during the competency assessment along

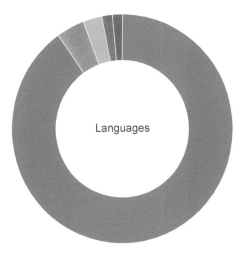

Figure 3.1.4. Proportion of language spoken in Baltimore

with sophisticated relational abilities.

2. Cultural adaptation - Adaptation to diverse cultural groups and exceptional behavioral skills dis-play when interacting with people from different cultures.

3. Tolerance practices - Discouragement of intolerance between individuals and groups with different cultural practices and beliefs

4. Informational Knowledge - Possesses exceptional knowledge about different ethnicity and races.

5. Stereotypical stand - Stereotypical eradication of cultural values and beliefs

6. Ethnic relationships and networking - Linkage of individuals among one another from different ethnic backgrounds

7. Self-awareness - Self-evaluation questionnaires for self-awareness and development

8. Participation - Cross-cultural event involvement and representation across different ethnicity and races.

Note:

1. A consistent standard for evaluation of competency should be applied to all candidates.

2. Competency assessment records

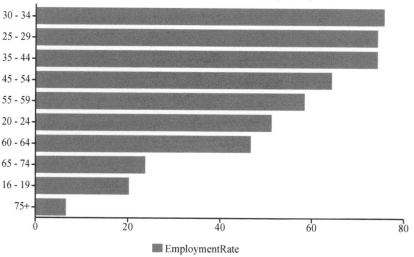

Figure 3.1.5. Employment rate by age in Baltimore

are retained for the entire time an individual is provided with the certification.

12.7.6. Competency assessment failure

1. If a candidate fails one or more areas of the competency assessment, the assessor will analyze the problem so that the proper corrective measures can be identified and implemented. Analysis of the problem starts with inspection of the protocols used for practice. The protocols should be clear and concise; if they are inadequate or confusing, this may account for the competency failure. In proficiency testing, it should be ensured that the proficiency sample is adequate and that a problem with the sample itself is not the cause of competency failure.

2. If the protocols are not the cause of the competency failure, the following questions should be answered: Did the candidate perform the test incorrectly (i.e., did he/she not follow the proper test procedure)? Did the candidate misunderstand the purpose or background of the performed test (i.e., is he/she unable to solve problems or adapt the test results to the clinical situation)? Did the candidate misunderstand the components of the test or instrument being used? Was the candidate unable to resolve QC problems? Did the candidate perform the test accurately but make an error in the documentation?

3. Discussion of the protocol with the candidate that fails competency is warranted to assess if further action is necessary, based on the candidate's verbal response. This may be sufficient to identify the reason for competency failure.

4. Actions that can be taken with an candidate who fails competency include: Having the candidate reread the protocol and discuss it with the supervisor in order to clarify any Having the candidate produce a flow chart to assist him or her in properly performing the protocol; Having the candidate observe another trained and competent candidate; Having the candidate practice the failed protocol with known specimens;

Having the candidate correctly retest the specimen originally tested during the failed competency assessment.

5. The reinstitution of formal training will be necessary if the above-mentioned methods fail to confirm that the candidate is competent.

6. Regardless of the selected corrective measures, it is necessary to repeat the competency assessment once the corrective measures have been completed. Successful accomplishment of competency for the a candidate who has failed the original competency assessment is to be documented.

7. Discussion of test and QC procedures in a quality assurance-QC meeting with all candidates could help sta to understand how certain types of errors can be avoided.

8. As a last resort, the candidate can be permanently removed from selected duties and reassigned to another work area.

12.8. Helping improve education statistics

12.8.1. Early childhood schooling

The early childhood environment

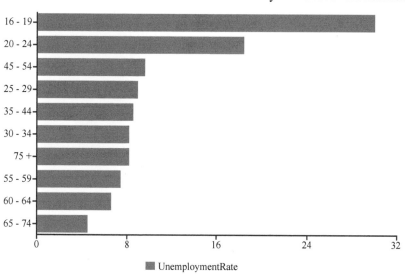

Figure 3.1.6. Unemployment rate by age in Baltimor

provides an opportunity to ensure that all children begin school "ready to learn ". It is well documented that early intervention assists in the child's growth and development. In this regard, kindergarten teachers and pre-school teachers are trained to listen for speech-language defects, problems, stuttering, articulation disorders, and slurred speech and help children accordingly. Thus, the sooner the child can receive services the better the prognosis.

5.8.1.1. Adequate supervision and training:

Early schooling enables students to receive some supervision and training in early childhood assessment and enhances their consultation and collaboration skills and prepares them for later assessments. Many of these individuals learn both expressive and receptive skills. This early documentation provides a foundational base-line for ascertaining if the child is improving in their vocabulary and skills and if the intervention has been fruitful. Contributing to the need for early education, research also shows that 15-year olds have better performance results in Programme for International Student Assessment (PISA) if they have had pre-primary education de-spite of socio-economic backgrounds.

5.8.1.2. Faster learning rate:

During the period from birth to 5 years of age, children undergo massive transformations in size, biological

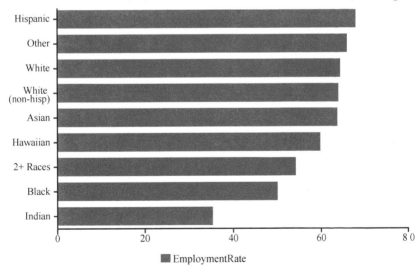

Figure 3.1.7. Employment rate by race in Baltimore

64

organization, behavioural capacities, and the social organization of experience that greatly complicate our understanding of the relation between culture and their learning processes. The first five years of a child's life are critical to his or her development. During this period, children learn at a faster rate than at any other time in their lives, developing cognitive, and social, and emotional skills that are fundamental to their achievements throughout child-hood and as adults. The rapid pace of development in early childhood means that investing in young children, both through their families and through access to

High-quality early childhood education and care leads to strong personal, social, and economic returns. Effective early learning also predicts positive well-being across a range of indicators in adulthood, including general well-being, physical and mental health, educational attainment, and employment. Disadvantaged children benefit from quality early childhood education and care the most, so investing in early childhood education and care and improving the quality of the environment for early development and learning could boost social mobility and inclusive growth.

12.8.2. 5.8.1.3. Interactive Opportunities:
An early learning environment that provides children with opportunities to engage in developmentally appropriate, stimulating, and language-rich activities and social interactions can compensate for the risks for children from disadvantaged backgrounds of falling behind or not reaching their full potential (Arnold and Docto-ro, 2003; Heckman, 2006). Research highlights the long-term benefits of investments in early childhood education and care programmes. Effective early learning also predicts well-being in adulthood across a range of indicators, including general wellbeing, physical and mental health, educational attainment, and employment. The areas of early learning that are of particular importance for many adult outcomes include: language and literacy; numeracy and other non-verbal cognitive skills; self-regulation; emotional health; social well-being; and social and emotional skills. During early learning, gains in one domain contribute to gains in others. This cycle of reinforcement across domains means that early learning programs should be assessed using a whole-child approach, recognizing the overlapping nature of outcomes for young children. A key goal of most governments' attempts to increase access to early childhood education and care is to improve equity in outcomes for older children and adults. This objective is also reflected in United Nations Sustainable

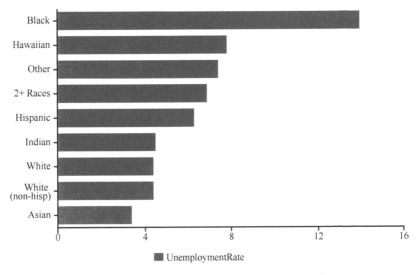

Figure 3.1.8. Unemployment rate by race in Baltimore

Development Goal 4.2: "Ensure that all children have access to quality early childhood education and care so that they are ready for primary education."

5.8.1.4. Cultural constraints

Many psychologists believe that children from different cultural groups learn a basic "cognitive style" characterized in somewhat different, but overlapping terms depending upon different scholarly traditions. One such "cognitive style" is said to privilege initial attention to the context in which events occur followed by attention to the objects that participate in the event; a similar formulation is between cultures that foster individualdualism or collectivism. It has been demonstrated, for example, that Japanese mothers asked to engage their 5-month-old child in an interaction involving an object, systematically orient the child to themselves first and to the object secondarily, whereas American mothers orient the child to the object first and themselves secondarily. At 5 months there is no difference discernable in the behavior of the children, but several months later, the children orient in the manner that has been shaped by repeated (differently-oriented) interactions with their parents in a wide variety of everyday events.

5.8.1.5. Cultural practices

Different forms of play (object play, symbolic play, and pretend role play) create different kinds of cultural environments for learning. However, there are wide cultural variations in the extent to which adults sanction different forms of play during early childhood. In societies where play is a valued cultural practice at this age, Poddiakov demonstrated how children carry out social experimentation with other persons in play and every-day life. Some researchers emphasize the importance of mutuality and transcending the present situation in play by creating other (imaginative) worlds. Vygotsky argued that distorting reality in play paradoxically reinforces learning applied to real-life by changing children's understanding of the relation between objects and meanings.

5.8.1.6. Brain's adaptation to change at different ages While most countries have clearly articulated curricula and well-established pedagogical approaches when it comes to primary and upper secondary education, there is much less agreement among and within countries on how best to build strong foundations in early childhood education and care in order to shift the emphasis from access to quality, and from care to quality education. There is also much debate over age-appropriate pedagogies and the right balance in the

Name	Total	In Poverty	Poverty Rate
Native	1,805	810	44.88%
Islander	286	103	36.01%
Other	9,988	2,967	29.71%
Black	376,479	99,663	26.47%
Hispanic	29,534	7,602	25.74%
Asian	14,860	3,070	20.66%
Multiple	13,244	2,653	20.03%
White	163,767	20,816	12.71%

Table 3.1.9. Poverty rate by race in Baltimore

development of cognitive, and social, and emotional competencies. Often the provision of early childhood education and care is highly fragmented within education systems. All of this has major implications for the initial and continuous professional development of sta, and for the work organization and governance of early childhood education and care.

While various factors influence children's learning, the home learning environment shapes their development the most (Figure). Families play a central nurturing and educational role, enriching their children's development through the activities they do together and other aspects of their home environment.

The family's influence is even stronger during a child's first two years when children need almost constant care, supervision, and timely and stimulating interaction. Children who experience fewer interactions with their parents (e.g. reading with children, number/letter activities, going to the library, painting and drawing, etc.) from ages 10 to 36 months perform lower on cognitive skills tests (e.g. in mathematics) later in life than children whose parents were more involved with them.

In 2012, among children under 6 years old who were not enrolled in kindergarten, the percentage who regularly received center-based care as their primary care arrangement was higher for Black (34 percent), Asian (33 percent), and White children (29 percent) than for Hispanic children (22 percent). In contrast, the percentage who regularly received home-based relative care as their primary care arrangement was higher for Hispanic 28 Preprimary, Elementary, and Secondary Education Participation children (23 percent) than for White (17 percent) and Asian children (16 percent); the percentage was also higher for Black children (25 percent) than for White and Asian children. The percentage of young children who regularly received home-based nonrelative care as their primary care arrangement was higher for White children (14 percent) than for Black (9 percent), Hispanic (8 percent), and Asian children (5 percent). The percentage was also higher for Hispanic than for

Asian children.

PISA 2015 found that 15-year-old students score four points higher in science for every additional year they had spent in pre-primary education, but the association largely disappears after accounting for the socioeconomic status of students and schools. One reason why the association is weak, even before accounting for the socio-economic profile of students and schools, is that the relationship is curvilinear: students who had spent less than one year in pre-primary education score lower in science than students who had not attended at all or who had spent more than one year.

12.8.3. Instructional Practices of Teachers, Participant in Professional Development and Career Satisfaction

Teachers play an important role in helping student's development and be educationally sound. Culture plays an essential role in how children make sense of the world. A decisive difference between children's learning and any intelligent technical system is that technical systems can recognize and organize information, but cannot grasp its meaning. Development of signification and adoption of the appropriate cultural tools (symbols, meanings, scripts, goals, etc.) of human activity are basic challenges of early learning.

New York City Median Age

New York City Sex Ratio

36.2	34.9	37.5			
			Female	4,480,165	52.34%
			Male	4,079,907	47.66%
Total	Male	Female			

It is necessary to remember that children do not make sense of the world consciously and analytically at this age. Meanings are grounded in bodily connections with things and are constantly bound up with the process of acting. Nonetheless, from birth or shortly thereafter, children are extremely sensitive to contingencies among all kinds of events in their environment. These range from learning characteristic patterns of activity, to the differential responses of people in their environment, to the contingencies among the phonemes in the language they hear that will form the basis of the grammar of their native language. Children are born already knowing the characteristic "tune" of their native language, learning that is displayed when different attention is given to vocalizations in that language. It is, therefore, necessary for teachers to indulge in Instructional Practices, professional development, and career satisfaction. Some of the ways this can be done are:

Teacher Clarity - When a teacher begins a new unit of study or project with students, he/she should clarify the purpose and learning goals, and provide explicit criteria on how students can be successful. It's ideal to also present models or examples to students so they can see what the end product looks like.

Classroom Discussion - Teachers need to frequently step o stage and facilitate the entire class discussion. This allows students to learn from each other. It's also a great opportunity for teachers to formatively assess (through observation) how well students are grasping new content and concepts.

Feedback - Along with individual feedback (written or verbal), teachers need to provide whole-group feedback on patterns they see in the collective class' growth and areas of need. Students also need to be given opportunities to provide feedback to the teacher so that she can adjust the learning process, materials, and instruction accordingly.

Formative Assessments - In order to provide students with effective and accurate feedback, teachers need to assess frequently and routinely where students are in relation to the unit of study's learning goals or end product (summative assessment). Teachers should spend the same amount of time on formative evaluation as they do on summative assessment.

Metacognitive Strategies - Students are given opportunities to plan and organize, monitor their own work, direct their own learning, and to self-reflect along the way. When we provide students with time and space to be aware of their own knowledge and their own thinking, student ownership increases. And research shows that metacognition can be taught.

Collaborating with colleagues - Great teachers are earnest learners and should spend time with a colleague, or two or three, and talk about what each of these research-based, best classroom practices looks like in the classroom. Discuss each one in the context of your unique learning environment: who your students are, what they need, what they already know, etc.

Anticipate possible responses to controversial topics. Students should be encouraged to openly share their views during discussions, but be prepared to correct stereotypes and challenge students' assumptions when comments are exchanged. It can be a di cult task to reconcile the tension between challenging offensive speech and not suppressing free speech. You should also consider your own response to emotion in the classroom and use this awareness to inform the planning process.

Include materials (readings, videotapes, etc.) that address underrepresented groups' experiences in ways that do not trivialize or marginalize these groups' experiences. Books that include a section on some aspect of diversity at the end of the text or books that highlight women, people of color, people with disabilities, gay men, lesbians, etc., inboxes and not in the body of the text can be seen as examples of the marginalization of these topics, groups, and group members' contributions. When it is important to use such books for other reasons, instructors have a responsibility to make students aware of the texts' limitations at the beginning of the course and to facilitate students' ability to read critically with these issues in mind.

The study of culture and early learning involves the interweaving of biological and cultural factors. Active development of subcultures aiming at expanding and enhancing learning is one promising current approach. But there is disagreement about what such subcultures should be. For example, play is only lately regaining the status of a legitimate form of learning activity.

Very important is the sheer exposure to the material to be learned that is an order by different cultural practices. It is a routine finding in research across many content domains that when children are asked to learn or solve problems based upon materials with which they are familiar, or in ways that make "human sense" they learn more rapidly.

These relations between culture and learning do not fade away but become even more pronounced as the children move from early into middle childhood and adolescence. Consequently, those concerned with leveraging the power of culture to promote learning should take care to pay as much attention to the cultural enrichment of children as to their health and physical well-being, all of which play an especially important role during this period of extraordinarily rapid developmental change.

Also, teaching satisfaction is a function of the perceived relation between what one wants from one's job and what one perceives teaching as offering or entailing. This is the product resulting from attitudinal and affective responses of teachers. That the level of job satisfaction of teachers is very high affects positively the educational aims come true. It is expected that a school that has teachers with a high level of job satisfaction gives qualified education and brings up successful students.

13. APPENDIX

1. US Central Bureau facts about the United States:
2. https://www.census.gov/quickfacts/fact/table/US/PST045218 City data of Detroit, Michigan of 2016: http://www.city-data.com/city/

Detroit-Michigan.html City data of Philadelphia of 2016: http://www.city-data.com/city/Philadelphia-Pennsylvania.html

3. City-data of New York City of 2016: http://www.city-data.com/city/New-York-New-York.html

4. City-data of Baltimore City of 2016: http://www.city-data.com/city/Baltimore-Maryland.html

5. City-data of Texas of 2016: http://www.city-data.com/city/Texas-City-Texas.html

6. US Central Bureau facts about Texas: https://www.census.gov/quickfacts/texascitycitytexas

Race	Population
White	3,661,800
Black or African American	2,081,507
Some Other Race	1,294,497
Asian	1,198,334
Two or More Races	285,089
American Indian and Alaska Native	34,487
Native Hawaiian and Other Pacific Islander	4,358

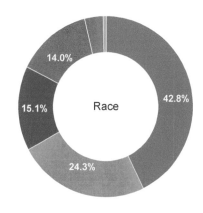

■ White   ■ Black or African American
■ American Indian and Alaska Native   ■ Asian
■ Native Hawaiian and Other Pacific Islander
■ Some Other Race   ■ Two or More Races

Figure 3.2.1. Proportion of people by race in New York

Name	Total	High School	Bachelors
White	2,088,693	1,939,182	1,198,497
Hispanic	1,580,472	1,057,532	274,459
Black	1,406,602	1,159,536	332,262
Asian	875,833	659,852	360,502
Other Race	798,339	507,255	108,403
Multiple Races	155,209	122,997	55,621
Native American	22,407	14,953	3,783
Islander	3,036	2,332	767

Table 3.2.2. Educational attainment in New York

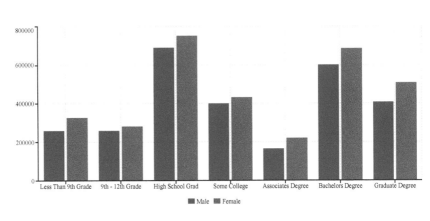

Figure 3.2.2. Educational attainment by gender in New York

Name	Total	High School	Bachelors
White	2,088,693	1,939,182	1,198,497
Hispanic	1,580,472	1,057,532	274,459
Black	1,406,602	1,159,536	332,262
Asian	875,833	659,852	360,502
Other Race	798,339	507,255	108,403
Multiple Races	155,209	122,997	55,621
Native American	22,407	14,953	3,783
Islander	3,036	2,332	767

Figure 3.2.3. Educational attainment by race in New York

■ Only English ■ Spanish ■ Other Indo-European ■ Asian ■ Other

Figure 3.2.2. The proportion of language spoken in New York

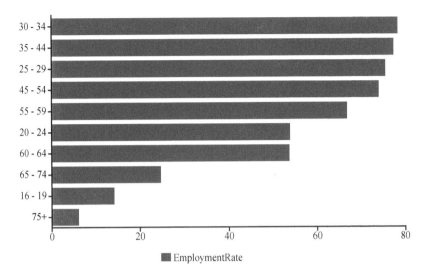

Figure 3.2.2. Educational attainment in New York

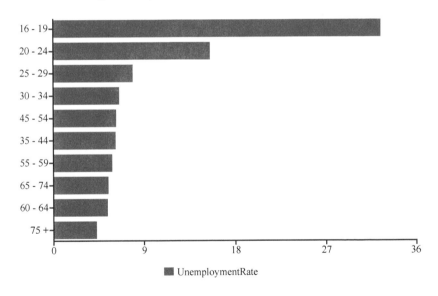

Figure 3.2.2. Educational attainment in New York

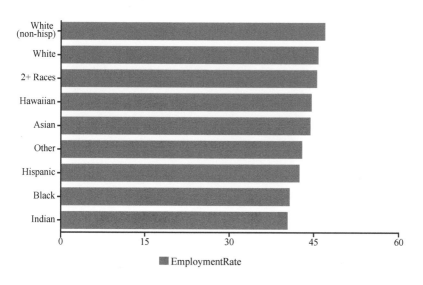

Figure 3.2.2. Educational attainment in New York

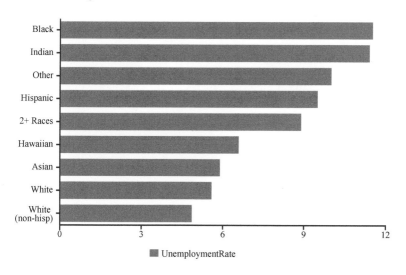

Figure 3.2.2. Educational attainment in New York

Name	Total	In Poverty	Poverty Rate
Other	1,281,025	388,935	30.36%
Native	34,003	9,411	27.68%
Hispanic	2,458,306	670,016	27.26%
Black	2,041,090	456,091	22.35%
Multiple	280,880	57,805	20.58%
Asian	1,185,902	219,041	18.47%
Islander	4,165	763	18.32%
White	2,695,034	320,801	11.90%

Table 3.2.9. Poverty rate by race

Philadelphia Sex Ratio

Female	827,245	52.70%
Male	742,412	47.30%

Philadelphia Median Age

34.1   32.6   35.5

Total   Male   Female

Race	Population
Black or African American	668,123
White	652,204
Asian	111,487
Some Other Race	87,384
Two or More Races	43,987
American Indian and Alaska Native	5,641
Native Hawaiian and Other Pacific Islander	831

Table 3.3.1. Population by Race in Philadelphia

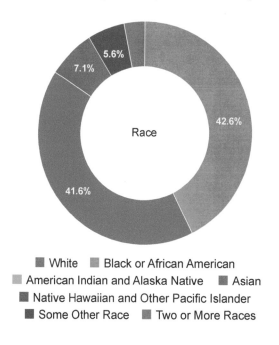

Figure 3.3.1. The proportion of people by race in Philadelphia

Education Attained	Count	Percentage
High School Graduate	355,809	33.82%
Some College	177,042	16.83%
Bachelors Degree	166,567	15.83%
Graduate Degree	118,269	11.24%
9th to 12th Grade	115,256	10.96%
Less Than 9th Grade	60,757	5.78%
Associates Degree	58,296	5.54%

Table 3.3.2. Educational attainment in Philadelphia

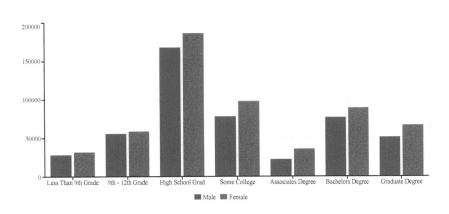

Figure 3.3.2. Educational attainment in Philadelphia

Name	Total	High School	Bachelors
Native	2,301	353,002	66,398
Multiple	12,598	382,182	169,677
Asian	9,536	77,702	15,741
Hispanic	51,124	52,195	27,740
BlacK	530,864	30,507	4,100
White	64,383	17,036	6,288
Other	20,353	2,685	731
Islander	102	407	137

Table 3.3.3. Educational attainment by race in Philadelphia

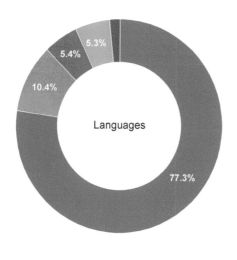

■ Only English ■ Spanish ■ Other Indo-European ■ Asian ■ Other

Figure 3.3.3. The proportion of languages spoken in Philadelphia

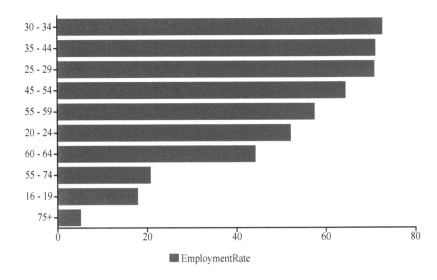

Figure 3.3.5. Employment by age in Philadelphia

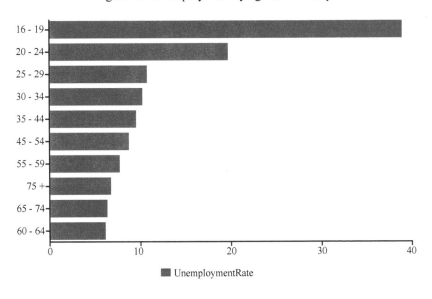

Figure 3.3.6. Unemployment by age in Philadelphia

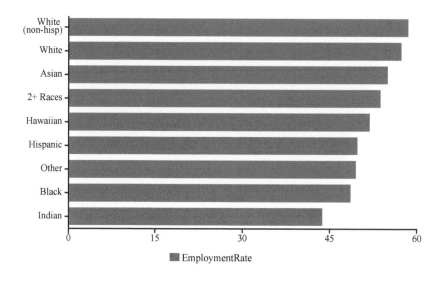

Figure 3.3.7. Employment by race in Philadelphia

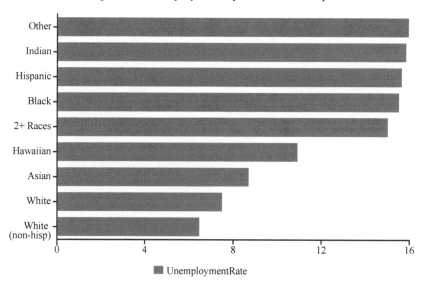

Figure 3.3.8. Unemployment by race in Philadelphia

Name	Total	In Poverty	Poverty Rate
Other	86,186	35,556	41.25%
Islander	819	332	40.54%
Hispanic	217,850	86,690	39.79%
Native	5,483	1,759	32.08%
Black	655,229	196,990	30.06%
Multiple	43,139	11,940	27.68%
Asian	107,338	28,698	26.74%
White	526,563	79,265	15.05%

Table 3.3.9. Poverty rate by race in Philadelphia

Texas Median Age

34.3   33.3   35.3

Total   Male   Female

Texas Sex Ratio

| Female | 13,802,635 | 50.34% |
| Male | 13,616,977 | 49.66% |

Race	Population
White	20,459,525
Black or African American	3,286,950
Some Other Race	1,580,393
Asian	1,236,852
Two or More Races	702,001
American Indian and Alaska Native	130,360
Native Hawaiian and Other Pacific Islander	23,531

Table 3.4.1. Population by race in Texas

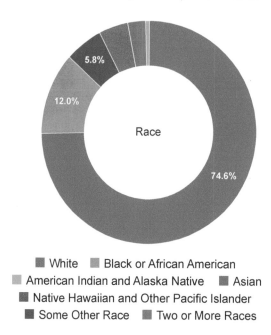

Figure 3.4.1. The proportion of the population by race in Texas

Education Attained	Count	Percentage
High School Graduate	4,372,430	25.05%
Some College	3,857,193	22.10%
Bachelors Degree	3,288,777	18.84%
Graduate Degree	1,721,618	9.86%
Less Than 9th Grade	1,513,995	8.67%
9th to 12th Grade	1,491,909	8.55%
Associates Degree	1,208,509	6.92%

Table 3.4.2. Educational attainment in Texas

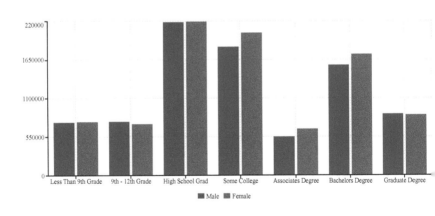

Figure 3.2.2. Educational attainment in Texas

Name	Total	High School	Bachelors
White	8,459,040	7,912,113	3,157,734
Hispanic	5,878,848	3,774,073	810,743
Black	2,047,741	1,812,812	474,431
Other Race	924,811	548,387	95,543
Asian	839,896	737,133	487,368
Multiple Races	293,365	253,709	89,319
Native American	82,415	64,598	15,713
Islander	14,794	13,171	2,990

Table 3.4.3. Educational attainment by race in Texas

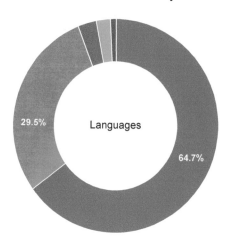

■ Only English ■ Spanish ■ Other Indo-European ■ Asian ■ Other

Figure 3.4.4. The proportion of Languages spoken in Texas

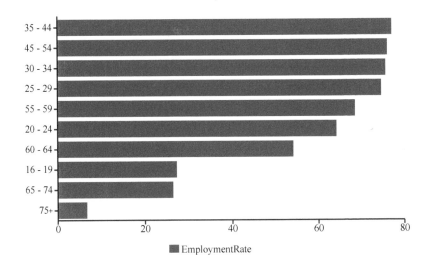

Figure 3.4.5. Employment by age in Texas

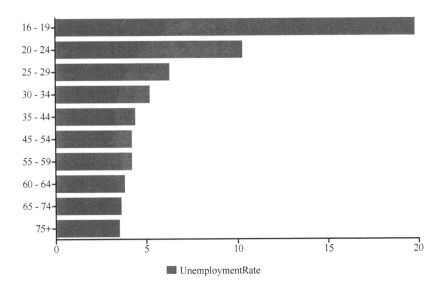

Figure 3.4.6. Unemployment by age in Texas

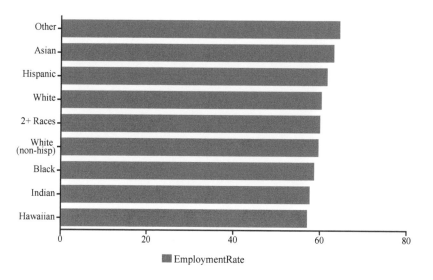

Figure 3.4.7. Employment by race in Texas

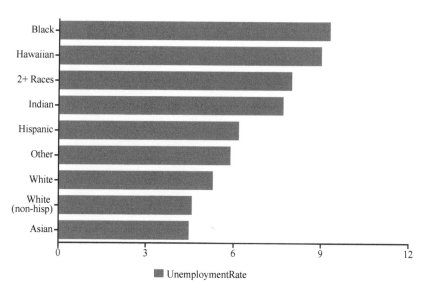

Figure 3.4.8. Unemployment by race in Texas

Name	Total	In Poverty	Poverty Rate
Hispanic	10,478,511	2,409,759	23.00%
Other	1,552,338	355,547	22.90%
Black	3,147,848	674,132	21.42%
Native	126,340	23,707	18.76%
Multiple	682,753	112,099	16.42%
Islander	22,763	3,449	15.15%
Asian	1,222,283	130,111	10.64%
White	11,492,426	1,016,351	8.84%

Table 3.4.9. Poverty rate by race in Texas

Detroit Median Age

34.7   32.8   36.5

Total   Male   Female

Detroit Sex Ratio

Female	358,524	52.73%
Male	321,341	47.27%

Race	Population
Black or African American	537,931
White	95,875
Some Other Race	20,527
Two or More Races	12,918
Asian	10,185
American Indian and Alaska Native	2,322
Native Hawaiian and Other Pacific Islander	107

Table 3.5.1. Population by Race in Detroit

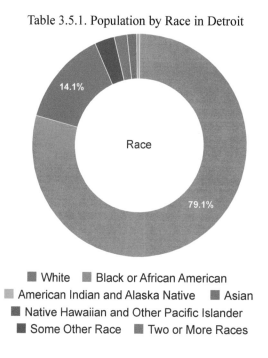

Figure 3.5.1. Proportion of people by race in Detroit

Education Attained	Count	Percentage
High School Graduate	141,431	32.65%
Some College	111,174	25.66%
9th to 12th Grade	62,839	14.51%
Bachelors Degree	36,765	8.49%
Associates Degree	31,086	7.18%
Less Than 9th Grade	25,010	5.77%
Graduate Degree	24,887	5.75%

Table 3.5.2. Educational attainment in Detroit

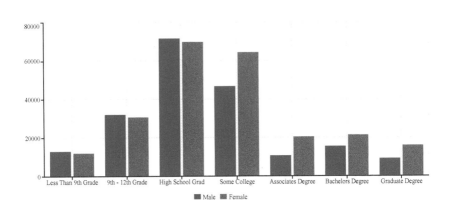

Figure 3.5.2. Educational attainment in Detroit

Name	Total	High School	Bachelors
Black	344,477	281,756	41,296
White	49,787	40,446	14,965
Hispanic	26,032	12,999	1,113
Other Race	10,722	5,043	380
Multiple Races	6,369	5,208	1,339
Asian	6,128	4,582	2,821
Native American	1,680	1,243	109
Islander	94	46	

Table 3.5.3. Educational attainment by race in Detroit

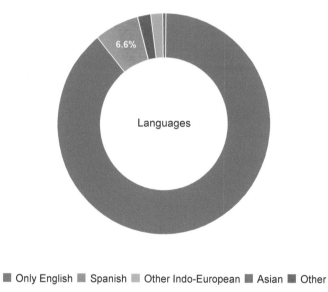

■ Only English ■ Spanish ■ Other Indo-European ■ Asian ■ Other

Figure 3.5.4. The language spoken by the proportion in Detroit

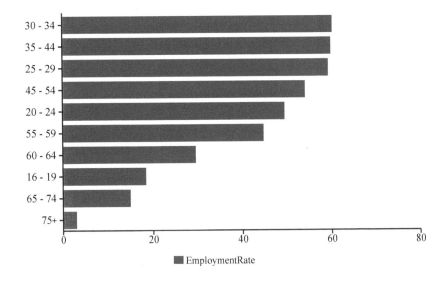

Figure 3.5.5. Employment by age in Detroit

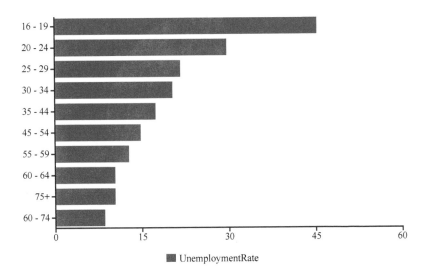

Figure 3.5.6. Unemployment by age in Detroit

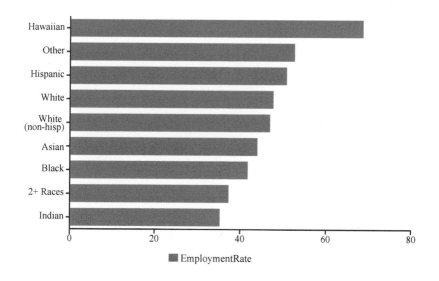

Figure 3.5.7. Employment by race in Detroit

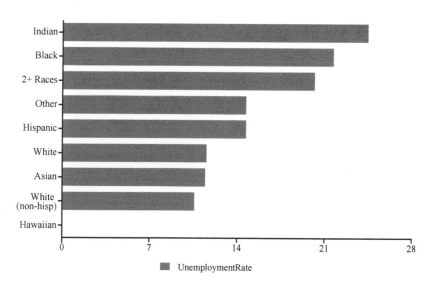

Figure 3.5.8. Unemployment by race in Detroit

Name	Total	In Poverty	Poverty Rate
Native	2,301	1,123	48.80%
Multiple	12,598	5,331	42.32%
Asian	9,536	4,001	41.96%
Hispanic	51,124	19,991	39.10%
BlacK	530,864	199,990	37.67%
White	64,383	23,558	36.59%
Other	20,353	7,360	36.16%
Islander	102	34	33.33%

Table 3.5.9. Poverty rate by race

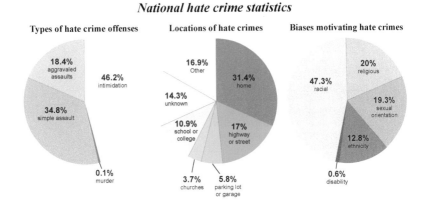

Figure 3.6. National hate crime statistics

Propartion of the nonelderly population who do not have a usual source of care, by race/ethnicity

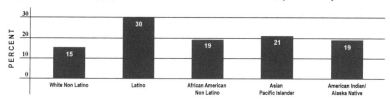

Figure 3.7.A. Proportion of non-elderly population who do not have a usual source of care, by race/ethnicity

FIGURE 3B

Propartion of the nonelderly population who are uninsured race/ethnicity

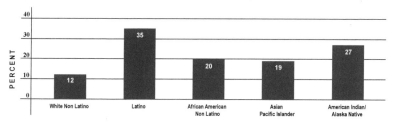

Figure 3.7.B. Proportion of non-elderly population who are uninsured, by race/ethnicity

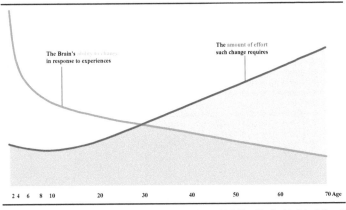

Source: C.A. Levitt (2009), *From Best Practices to Breakthrough Impacts: A Science-Based Approach to Building a More Promising Future for Young Children and Families*, Center on the Developing Child, Harvard University, Cambridge, MA.

Figure 5.8.1.a. The Brain's Ability to Change and
The Amount of Eﬀort Required For Such Change

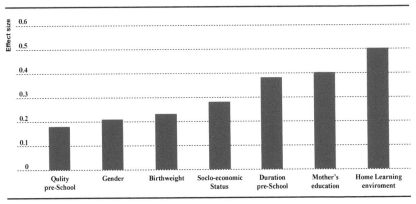

Note: Effect size compares the relative strength of different factors that influence children's literacy proficiency at age 5. It is expressed in the units of standard deviations where an effect of 0.1 is relatively weak, one of 0.40 is moderately strong, and an effect of 0.70 is strong.

Source: Melhuish, E. et al., (2008), "Effects of the home learning environment and preschool center experience upon literacy and numeracy development in early primary school", Journal of Social Issues, No.64, pp.95-114.

Figure 5.8.1.b. Impact of Contextual Factors on Children's Literacy at Age 5

Percent

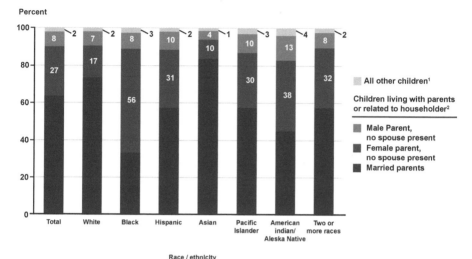

Figure 5.8.1.c. Percentage distribution of children under age 18, by race/ ethnicity and living arrangement: 2016

References

1. Banks, J. (1995). Multicultural education: Historical development, dimensions, and practice. In J. A. Banks, & C. A.

2. McGee Banks (Eds.), Handbook of research on multicultural education (pp. 3–49). New York: Macmillan.

3. Baron, W. (2006). Confronting the challenging working conditions of new teachers: What mentors and induction programs can do. In B. Achinstein, & S. Z. Athanases (Eds.), Mentors in the making: Developing new leaders for new teachers (pp. 125–135). New York: Teachers College Press.

4. Bennett, C. I. (2002). Enhancing ethnic diversity at a big ten university through Project TEAM: A case study in teacher education. Educational Researcher, 31(2), 21–29.

5. Bhawuk, D. P. S., Sakuda K. H., y Munusamy V. P. (2008) Inter-cultural competence development and triple loop cultural learn-ing. En Soon Ang inn Van Dyne Handbook of cultural intelligence; theory measurement and application, Armonk, NY: M. E Shape. (342–345).

6. Athanases, Steven & Martin, Kathleen. (2006). Learning to Advocate for Educational Equity in a Teacher Credential Program. Teaching and Teacher Education. 22. 627–646. 10.1016/j.tate.2006.03.008.

7. Blank RM, Dabady M, Citro CF, eds. Measuring Racial Dis-crimination. Washington, DC: National Academies Press; 2004.

8. Bronheim S, Goode T. Documenting the Implementation of Cultural and Linguistic Competence: Guide for Maternal and Child Health Bureau Funded Training Programs. Washington, DC: National Center for Cultural Competence, Georgetown University Center for Child and Human Development; 2013.

9. Culture and Conflict Resolution, John Folk-Williams, March 28, 2010, http:// www.crosscollaborate.com/2010/03/culture-conflict-resolution/

10. Cross Cultural Awareness in Conflict Resolution j Negotiation Skills, July 17, 2019 https://www.notredameonline.com/resources/intercultural-management/ cross-cultural-awareness-may-aide-your-conflict-resolution-eorts/

11. The Importance of Early Childhood Education, Micheal F. Shaughnessy, January 2012 https://www.researchgate. net/publication/233763048_The_Importance_of_ Early_Childhood_Education

12. Teacher's Job Satisfaction Levels, Zulf'u" Demirtau,´ 2010 https://www. sciencedirect.com/science/article/pii/S187704281002392X

13. Heckman, J. (2006), "Skill formation and the economics of in-vesting in disadvantaged children" , Science, Vol. 312/5782, pp. 1900-1902, http://dx.doi. org/10.1126/science.1128898

14. Arnold, D. and G. Doctoro (2003), "The early education of socioeconomically disadvantaged children", Annual Review of Psychology, Vol. 54/1, pp. 517-545, http://dx.doi.org/10.1146/annurev.psych.54.111301.145442.

CPSIA information can be obtained
at www.ICGtesting.com
Printed in the USA
LVHW070350210221
679527LV00002B/43